Advance praise for *The New Devil's Dictionary:*

"Ambrose Bierce's original *Devil's Dictionary* defined basic truths in such a way as to surprise, shock, infuriate, and, not infrequently, delight his readers. Rhoda Koenig's wonderful reprise attains that high standard again and again."
JOHN BERENDT
author of *Midnight in the Garden of Good and Evil*

"The devil is a woman, as movie director Josef von Sternberg and Marlene Dietrich once insisted, and Rhoda Koenig proves it. *The New Devil's Dictionary* is bracing, provoking, often brilliant—I ran from one entry to another and was constantly amused and amazed."
DAVID DENBY
author of *Snark*

"This updated version of Ambrose Bierce's *Devil's Dictionary* is so smart and mordant it must be read slowly and savored. A great idea, brilliantly executed."
ANDREW HOLLERAN
author of *Dancer from the Dance*

The New
DEVIL'S
DICTIONARY

The New
DEVIL'S
DICTIONARY

A NEW VERSION OF THE CYNICAL CLASSIC

RHODA KOENIG
Illustrations by Peter Breese

LYONS PRESS
GUILFORD, CONNECTICUT
An imprint of Globe Pequot Press

Copyright © 2012 by Rhoda Koenig
Illustrations copyright © 2012 by Peter Breese

Lyons Press is an imprint of Globe Pequot Press.

Text design by Sheryl Kober
Page layout by Sue Murray and Melissa Evarts

Library of Congress Cataloging-in-Publication Data is available on file.

ISBN 978-0-7627-7247-6

Printed in the USA

10 9 8 7 6 5 4 3 2 1

Introduction

In a land where the right to pursue happiness has become a duty, and where pessimism is regarded as lack of patriotism, the cynic—or truth-teller, as some call him—has always had a rough ride. The little boy who points out that the emperor is naked may be a fairy-tale hero, but anyone who proclaims a real-life hero a fraud had better have him dead to rights or have one foot out the door.

Ambrose Bierce was often on the move. He was born in 1842, the tenth of thirteen children in a family he described as "unwashed savages." Bierce's father, an Indiana farmer and whimsical sadist, gave each of his sons and daughters a name beginning with "A," creating a good beginning for a lexicographer but doubtless many trying moments for Ambrose, Almeda, Aurelia, et al. Bierce left home at fifteen to become a printer's apprentice. A few years later, he enlisted in the Civil War, in which he twice risked his life rescuing wounded men and suffered a head wound that long afterward caused him pain and fainting fits. His experiences were the raw material for such stories as "An Occurrence at Owl Creek Bridge" and "What I Saw at Shiloh." This was the first fiction to portray war not as a glorious crusade but as a nightmare of incompetence and madness in which survival and even heroism are often achieved by nothing more heroic than dumb luck. Nevertheless, a taste—or disregard—for danger would seem necessary for Bierce's next positions as a federal agent in the postwar South, where he narrowly escaped death in a shootout with veterans who "did not consider themselves included in the surrender," and as a member of a surveying party in Indian Territory (now eastern Oklahoma).

The last stop in Bierce's government service was San Francisco, where he decided to return to private life. Rough yet cosmopolitan, the city of 1866 suited him, and its lively newspapers and literature—Bret Harte and Mark Twain were beginning to win national recognition— appealed to his combative spirit. Bierce supplemented his sketchy education by reading Swift, Voltaire, and other favorites of the disaffected, and he began contributing satirical pieces to local publications. In just two years, with his "Town Crier" column in the *News-Letter*, the twenty-six-year-old Bierce was not only the best-known journalist in San Francisco but was quoted in New York and London for his audacity and his misanthropic, often macabre wit. Bierce ridiculed artists without talent, politicians without honor—the epitaph of one of the latter, he said, should be "Here lies Frank Pixley, as usual"—and all manifestations of religion: "On last Sunday afternoon a Chinaman passing guilelessly along Dupont Street was assailed with a tempest of bricks and stones from the steps of the First Congregational Church. At the completion of this devotional exercise the Sunday-scholars retired within . . . to hear about Christ." Many of Bierce's comments, such as those on political corruption in California, were not opinions but statements of fact, leading to so many threats on his life that he wore a revolver to work.

In 1875, the San Francisco *Argonaut* ran a list of Bierce's satirical definitions. He used the idea twice more but did not pursue it steadily until 1881, when he became editor of a weekly that might have been named for him: *The Wasp.* There he wrote an intermittent series titled "The Devil's Dictionary," which he continued under the name "The Cynic's Dictionary" after moving to the *Examiner* in 1887. These comic definitions, a form he invented, did nothing to soften his reputation. Among them were "Lawyer: One skilled in circumvention of the law" and "Husband: One who, having dined, is charged with the care of the plate." He defined a cynic as "a blackguard whose faulty vision sees things as they are, not as they ought to be," a sardonic defense of the truth-teller that contradicts Oscar Wilde's more famous definition—"one who knows the price of everything and the value of nothing." But Bierce, sadly, was proved right about the wisdom of acknowledging reality: Wilde would have escaped prison, ruin, and an early death had he not let himself believe that his charm and fame made him invulnerable to British law and public opinion. Expecting the worst, cynics are seldom caught napping.

Though labeled "Bitter Bierce" by those who did not know him, Bierce did not fit the stereotype of a cynic—a crabbed and twisted man sulking in corners. Tall, handsome, and amusing, married to a beautiful and wealthy woman, he had a harem of ladies to whom he was teacher, patron, and sometimes lover. A male friend, praising his kindness and unselfishness, said Bierce "would have given his coat to his bitterest enemy who happened to be cold." Any cynic, however, is destined to be resented and misrepresented by those who ignore the deceits and cruelties of daily life, who consider them unpleasant but necessary, or who transform them into virtues. The cynic's insistent questions and contradictions annoy the conventional, who characterize him as a reflexive naysayer or an overage child. This may be the case with the adolescent kind— most teenagers become cynics for a time upon discovering the wickedness of the world and its lack of interest in them—but the lifelong cynic has deeper concerns than embarrassing his elders. He wants to make his fellow citizens stare into the abyss between principles and practice, to shame them onto the path of righteousness, as Bierce did by excoriating the brick-throwing churchgoers: Having encouraged immigration for the backbreaking, underpaid work of building the railroads, white Californians wanted the Chinese to disappear once it was done.

Nor did Bierce fit the popular image of the cynic as a man who is all talk. In 1896, enraged by the prospect that Congress would pass a bill absolving railroad magnate Collis P. Huntington of his $75 million debt to the government, Bierce traveled to Washington and campaigned so furiously that Huntington tried to bribe him to stop. Asked his price, Bierce said it was $75 million, payable to "my friend the Treasurer of the United States." The bill was defeated, a great victory for Bierce, who had for many years attacked the Western robber barons and their trains, which, he said, were frequently dangerous and so late that "passengers were exposed to the perils of senility before arriving at their destinations."

Bierce moved from one San Francisco publication to another, his tenure often shortened by his attacks on their owners, one of whom was so terrorized that he sold the paper for fear that trying to curb his star writer would incite him to worse abuse. By 1908, Bierce was no longer an editor or even a staff writer. He was living in Washington, D.C., long separated from his wife. His two beloved sons had died, one by his own hand after killing the man who had eloped with his fiancée. Paternal love did not make Bierce any more reverent of the remains of the dead than he was of the ashes of a friend, a fellow critic, which he suggested be molded into bullets and fired at publishers. Bierce kept his son's ashes on his desk in a cigar box.

When a publisher proposed to rescue Bierce's finances and reputation with a twelve-volume edition of his collected works, Bierce set about editing, but, worried and suffering from severe asthma as well as the lingering effects of the Civil War head wound, he succumbed to the vanity he had always ridiculed in others. Twelve volumes were too many for a writer whose best work was, if sharp as a needle, also as slender as one. They were bulked out by pieces written in journalistic haste, dated and repetitious. Reviews praising the short stories and the volume published in 1911 as *The Devil's Dictionary* were outnumbered by weary dismissals of the rest.* Sales were also limited by the publisher's high-handed refusal to sell the volumes separately. The times were against Bierce as well. America

---

* Only two years later another milestone in the history of cynicism was published—Gustave Flaubert's *Dictionary of Received Ideas*, which, like Bierce's work, was a collection of observations that its author had made in his last thirty years. Flaubert's received ideas are platitudes and banalities, automatic remarks that make up so much of conversation. Forming a bulwark against intellect and passion, they are indispensable, said Flaubert, to anyone who would be considered a decent and likable member of bourgeois society. Some examples: Blondes: Sexier than brunettes, Censorship: Has its uses, no matter what people say, Gift: "It's the thought that counts." A stranger, mistaking Flaubert for someone else, asked if he was a salesman of oil. "No," said Flaubert. "Vinegar."

was still mainly rural and conservative. The Gilded Age—when new and huge wealth was its own justification and social Darwinists saw no wrong in massacring Indians, lynching blacks, and grinding the poor—still cast a long shadow. Americans were not sympathetic to a critic of their morals, no matter how witty.

The failure of his bid for posterity as well as Bierce's other problems have led many to believe that his last adventure was a version of "suicide by cop"—creating a situation in which someone else is obliged to pull the trigger. "To be a Gringo in Mexico," he wrote, "—oh, that is euthanasia!" In 1913, at the age of 71, he told friends he was going to observe the Mexican Revolution, then in progress. "If you should hear of my being stood up against a Mexican stone wall and being shot to rags, please know that I think it is a pretty good way to depart this life. It beats old age, disease, or falling down the cellar stairs." His last letter, from San Antonio on December 26, 1913, ended, "I leave here tomorrow for an unknown destination." It still is. Bierce's date of death is traditionally given as "1914?" but no one knows where or how he ended up.

Not long after Bierce died, literary fashion turned once again from tradition to rebellion, and the miasma of sentiment began to lift. The revulsion from an authority that had squandered so many lives in World War I, the growing maturity of literature and journalism inspired by iconoclasts such as H. L. Mencken, and the gaily irreverent humor of the Twenties made a receptive audience for Bierce. In 1925, *The Devil's Dictionary* was reprinted, and in 1929 four books about Bierce were published. Thereafter his popularity has steadily, if quietly, grown; editions adding material from Bierce's journalism have been published, the most exhaustive appearing in 2000. The *Dictionary* has become a minor classic, each generation appreciating what it finds most relevant. While the cheeky Twenties laughed at such definitions as "Bacchus: A convenient deity invented by the ancients as an excuse for getting drunk," and its feminists liked "Bride: A woman with a fine prospect of happiness behind her," the Thirties smiled grimly at "Air: A nutritious substance supplied by a bountiful Providence for the fattening of the poor" and "Labor: One of the processes by which A acquires property for B."

In prosperous times, Bierce's certainty that ignorance, arrogance, and greed pull the levers of society can be scorned as the mutterings of a loser and spoilsport. In times like the present, that's not so easy. The failure of our legal and economic systems to prevent disaster and the disregard for ordinary prudence and foresight have made us uncomfortably aware that we cannot trust those in charge either for compassion or competence. Recent events have made some of these century-old definitions uncomfortably pertinent. The last three presidential elections have made more relevant than ever Bierce's observation that a president is someone whom immense numbers of his countrymen did not want for president. Baby boomers, whose rebellious spirits chimed with Bierce's when they were young in the Sixties, are now old enough to have become cynics through experience rather than ideology. In between, they, like most, reject the cynic. From their mid-twenties to late middle age, people are less susceptible to cynicism than the young, who are shocked at the iniquities of mankind, and the old, who have seen and suffered so many of them. The hope, energy, and egotism necessary to carry out the world's work tend to dampen the belief that it may, even if successful, not be worthwhile. And since one cannot raise a child to believe that all adults are rogues and fools and that all endeavor is doomed, a parent must refuse to believe it, too, or at least try to give that impression.

A hundred years on, Bierce's cold eye and diamond-tipped pen retain their ability to shock and amuse. But some of his definitions are now about as shocking as the sight of a female knee, and, in 1911, one topic, highly productive of vice and folly, could hardly be mentioned at all. Many of Bierce's opinions, such as his opposition to women's suffrage, sound less cynical than mean-spirited. And of course the past century—sometimes, it seems, the past week—has seen an explosion of idiotic behavior, beliefs, and words. A new dictionary, therefore, seemed in order. Like the original, this version includes eternal abstractions, fashionable imbecilities, and words that are used without regard to their implicit fatuity or chicanery. Bierce illustrated many definitions with his own poems and parodies, which were sometimes witty but more often, in the style of his time, laboriously facetious. The examples in this version are taken from the author's experience, newspaper reports, and works of fiction and philosophy that show the forms that cynicism has taken, as books for children say, through the ages and in many lands. As in Bierce's dictionary, no one is spared, not even the reader. "Self-esteem," he wrote, in a definition that would horrify the schoolmarms of our time, was "an erroneous appraisement."

In a time of wars, economic gloom, family breakdown, and other daily miseries, won't a book based on the idea of universal stupidity and venality make people even more unhappy? That was never the case with Bierce or with any true cynic, whose view is one of amused detachment. "Out of the spectacle of life about him," said H. L. Mencken, "he got an unflagging and Gargantuan joy. The obscene farce of politics delighted him. He was an almost amorous connoisseur of theology and theologians. He howled with mirth whenever he thought of a professor, a doctor, or husband." One may not wish to be a cynic all the time, but being aware of the absurdities of life can make its sorrows easier to bear. Detachment also enables us to step out of the path of the juggernaut driven by international capitalism. It often seems that, by a coincidence whose effects are as severe as if they were the result of collusion, the aim of commerce and government is to make us all into ideal consumer-citizens—ignorant, passive, nervous, confused, at the mercy of our artificially inflated appetites and the latest fad or fear. But detachment need not mean removal from the fray; it can be, rather, the coolness of the doctor or soldier who must destroy to do good, of the preacher who loves the sinner but hates the sin.

In recent years, we have seen an increase in a vulgar and superficial kind of cynicism, a notion that coarseness and contempt are expressions of frankness and independence. As Bierce's life shows, however, true cynicism means having nobler values than the liars and crooks, not caving in to their contempt for us. But it also means, painful as that may be, acknowledging the stains on our own record of intelligence and virtue. That is why this dictionary sets out to demolish the complacency of liberal and conservative, rich and poor, male and female, old and young. Armed with knowledge and self-knowledge, as well as ideals, we can start putting the heat on those who give us most reason to be cynical.

The New
DEVIL'S
DICTIONARY

absolution *n.* Start of a new round of sinning.

academia *n.* Staging post on the way to adulthood, where visitors learn how to make others believe they know something from inhabitants who are convinced they do.

academic *n.* Person engaged in questions or practices relating to academia, i.e. those on which reality has little or no bearing. An academic can spend thirty years examining an author's motives and influences without considering whether he is any good, an approach the academic is not likely to apply to his wife.

accessible *adj.* (1) Of a subject, one that can be approached by the most intellectually handicapped, aided by the ramp of banality and the guardrail of diminished vocabulary. (2) Of a woman, a nice way of putting it.

actually *adv.* (1) Genteel cough of propitiation at failure to meet expectations: "I haven't actually got to that yet" conveys the idea that, while the speaker has not performed the work, he or she has been thinking about it, if only how to get out of doing it, and therefore deserves a degree of credit. (2) Attempt to soften a horrible but undeniable fact. From an obituary of Baroness Park: "Her father . . . never actually married her mother." (3) Gasp of awe at someone's performing a natural or necessary activity: "To prepare for the role, he actually read several books on the subject."

adequate *adj.* Insufficient. Disappointment at actual compared with imagined recompense for financial or emotional outlay is inevitable with marriage, investments, and portion sizes.

adult *n.* Person who, unlike a child, anticipates the consequences of an act and accepts responsibility and, if applicable, punishment. A definition that remains largely theoretical, as anyone knows who has tried to explain it to a thirty-year-old in a T-shirt proclaiming the wearer naughty but cute.

adultery *n.* Sauce that, on goose or gander, makes a tasty dish to set before the lawyer.

advertiser *n.* The only person allowed, in a sensitive world, to suggest that you are in some way inadequate, as he can provide an instant remedy.

With the individual now encouraged to find success by becoming a product ("Brand yourself!"), we have now all become advertisers, pointing out to anyone who can't escape quickly enough the distinctive and admirable qualities of Me, Inc.

advise *v.* To urge someone of different tastes, temperament, and financial standing to proceed in the way you found successful twenty years ago.

affordable *adj.* Of an item whose price is, for the lower class, impossible; for the upper class, inconsiderable. The middle class can afford it only with difficulty, but to admit as much would be contemptible.

ageism *n.* Discrimination against the old in the belief that they are unaware of or hostile to recent developments, have difficulty getting along with younger people, are fixated on trivialities, repeat long and boring anecdotes from thirty or forty years ago, and are forgetful, slow, and obstinate. It is not known how ideas so erroneous have become so widespread.

aging *adj., n.* Living. Process that begins at birth but is popularly considered to start only when one's hair turns white—or, as it is always called, gray. These are just two of the numerous euphemisms and falsehoods, such as "golden years," that accompany one from middle age to the grave.

The correct word, for which "aging" substitutes, is "aged," an adjective thought less likely to indicate accrued value in humans than in wine and cheese.

alertness *n.* Quality indispensable for self-preservation. See obliviousness.

altruism *n.* The belief that one's efforts on another's behalf will produce a better result than doing nothing. Often found in combination with the belief that, when one rings the doorbell, the inhabitants are away rather than hiding. See charity.

anti-Semite *n.* Literally one who dislikes Jews and Arabs. As hostility always trumps accuracy, in practice it is one who dislikes only Jews, even if he does so for irritating qualities not unique to them, such as enriching themselves through the labor of others. In preindustrial countries, millers were often deeply resented for, as the farmers saw it, turning a profit in a few hours from what they had taken months to grow. So it is possible for anti-Semitism to exist without Jews, though of course it is much more fun with them.

apology *n.* **(1)** From governments and corporations, a statement of praise for the organization ("We have fallen from our usually high standards") and a clarification of its purpose ("It was not our intention to offend"). **(2)** From individuals, an expression of indifference, often one of the rare statements of negative emotion ("I'm not proud of what I did"). **(3)** On behalf of the dead, a statement of regret so sincere as to obviate the need for reparations.

arguably *adv.* Probably not. Used by those too ignorant, lazy, or timid to make an argument but wishing more gravitas than can be conferred by "perhaps."

aristocracy *n.* A fragmented nation, not because its members were subject to a diaspora but because those in each country sprang up independently. The aristocrat may complain, as much as the laborer, of excessive immigration, but his countrymen are found in the castles and villas of foreign countries whose inhabitants also possess, with a serenity too deep for smugness, one of the few things that cannot be bought: the past. In a sense, they are the truest egalitarians: To them, everyone not of their number, whether a college president or a derelict shaking coins in a paper cup, is on the same level. The classic expression of the aristocrat's deracinated condition is the remark made to a visitor by the English owner of an Elizabethan mansion, at whose gates stood the cottages of a dozen villagers: "We're quite isolated here, you know. We haven't any neighbors for twenty miles."

art *n.* Drawing, painting, and sculpture, which, by allowing self-expression and radiating beauty, promote virtue and happiness, as may be seen in the characters of artists, art collectors, art teachers, art dealers, art curators, art historians, and art critics.

art for art's sake *n.* Doctrine that sought to counter the idea that art should serve a purpose, such as telling a story or praising virtue. Now obsolete, as it is recognized that the sole purpose of art is to contribute to the artist's, purchaser's, and dealer's wealth and social standing.

assimilation *n.* Means by which immigrants can become less irritating to the inhabitants of their new country, at the same time making themselves happier and more successful. Some of the most backward, however, sadly resist it. Many Muslim parents in England and America, for example, refuse to raise their daughters in the manner of non-Muslims, even though the intellect, charm, and discretion of young women in these countries are the envy of the world.

attention span *n.* Maximum time the average person can concen

average man *n.* Person of below-average intelligence. The wealthy and famous humorist P. J. O'Rourke tells his readers he is, like them, an average man; they believe him.

avuncular *adj.* Like an uncle. Protective without being possessive, benevolent without sowing guilt, disappointed without being angry, affectionate without—but perhaps we should remember that this definition was not created by an aunt who returned home early after leaving her husband alone with his niece.

awakening *n.* Daily triumph of hope over experience.

baby talk *n.* Discourse of people old enough to have babies—or grown children—of their own. Used to emphasize one's affection or sensitivity ("the n-word") in the absence of evidence.

balance *n.* In journalism or gossip, the countering of a statement, no matter how factual, with a contrary view, no matter how feeble, on the basis that being hit with a pound of feathers feels the same as being hit with a pound of lead.

based *part.* Word that implies a more exciting activity than mere living ("I'm based in New York").

bathroom *n.* Public place to which Americans request directions when they wish to urinate or defecate. Also referred to as "restroom." Provokes amused condescension from the English, who do not pretend to bathe or rest when performing a natural function of which no one need be ashamed, and instead ask discreetly for a place to wash, or lavatory.

battle *n.* Protracted terminal illness. A locution that, to spare the relatives any guilt for inattention or economy, suggests that the sufferer was not helpless and terrified but fighting fit and just didn't fight hard enough to vanquish those cancer cells.

beauty *n.* Quality that, in inanimate objects, arouses resentment and rage, therefore discouraged and scorned by civic planners and artists. In women, the prejudice in its favor remains, but the proponents of diversity and democracy have made it less of an accolade. A woman described as "not conventionally beautiful" is understood to be one whose face would stop a clock.

bed and breakfast *n.* Establishment run by a couple whom others pay to enjoy the discomforts of home.

best man *n.* The man who won and does not have to marry the bride.

big *adj.* Way to describe a fat man who might buy something.

biography *n.* Literary work that nearly always leaves one thinking less of its subject. On learning the details of Jean-Paul Sartre's life, one is left in no doubt that his observation "Hell is other people" is on the money if one of them is Jean-Paul Sartre.

The novel or collection of essays is usually an inadvertent autobiography or at least a psychological profile, a fact sadly ignored by the wives of Philip Roth and Norman Mailer.

birth-control pill *n.* Contraceptive that has ensured that every baby born since its invention has been wanted—by its mother.

blasphemy *n.* Act that enables us to raise our status from a mere petitioner of the deity to his friend. The emperor Tiberius denounced this pretension by saying, "Offenses against the gods are the gods' business," but he was a pagan, so what did he know.

body *n.* Carapace of the soul, admired in no matter what form, by artists, whose business it is to do so, and by the owner, who will delude himself for free. For a true estimate of the artist's idea of beauty, do not look at his sitters but at his wife.

boo *interj.* Cry announcing the presence of a ghost, theatergoer of high standards, or other imaginary being.

boobs *n.* (1) Snappy term for secondary sexual characteristics whose primary purposes of attraction and infant nutrition have been superseded, now that they may be altered to fit the demands of the marketplace, by that of vanity or financial enrichment. (2) Those providing the enrichment.

bore *n.* One whose mistaken self-regard arises from being such a bad listener that he never bores himself.

{boo}

{bottle}

bottle *n.* Vessel from which its owner is seldom parted, containing, in infancy, milk necessary for survival, and, in adulthood, branded water vital for social credibility.

bright *n.* Of a child, not actually retarded. Of a room, in real-estate parlance, minuscule.

{Canadian}

C
D

calorie *n.* Unit attesting to the innumeracy of many and the puritanism of many others. The diner who counts calories, said a famous cook, is like a lover who, in bed, wears a wristwatch.

campaign *n.* Political courtship during which the reasons adduced to vote for a candidate are as trustworthy as preludes to urgent seduction. "Those ain't lies," protests the candidate's manager in the film *Hail the Conquering Hero* when his whoppers are challenged. "Those are campaign promises."

Canadian *n.* Person who is angered rather than flattered at being taken for an American.

capital *n.* Word meaning "money" or "excellent." Lexical coincidence.

capital punishment *n.* Excellent means of expending on the legal profession the money that could be squandered on a prisoner's maintenance and rehabilitation. Multimillionaires whose financial creativity drives several people to suicide never share the fate of those physically responsible for the demise of only one—yet another example of the prejudice against manual labor.

care *v., n.* On its own ("I care about this/you"), a way for the speaker to assert dominance while appearing selfless. In compound form ("caregiver," "foster care," "care in the community"), a guarantee of cruelty or indifference.

casual *adj.* Of sex, haphazard. Of clothing, the type that favors the wearer's comfort over the viewer's pleasure. It is not surprising that the characteristics of the second category influence the success of the first. If a man considers buttons too much trouble, he is usually a bad bet for foreplay.

Catholicism *n.* Religion based on cannibalism of a man long dead that seeks to prevent the death of those not yet born.

celebrity *n.* One, temporarily enjoying a state of beatitude, whose number has increased to meet demand. Kings were once erroneously thought capable of curing disease at a touch; the celebrity, however, by addressing another by name, can indeed heal the scrofula of nonentity.

The eighteenth-century French playwright Count Villiers de l'Isle-Adam wrote that the purpose of servants was to do our living for us. In the present, more democratic age, celebrities fulfill this function, allowing us to reserve our efforts for everything else.

Being the friend of a celebrity has not always been regarded as an unmixed blessing, as indicated by this caption to a 1901 cartoon: "How many celebrities do you know, and what does it cost you?"

cell phone *n.* Invention that has brought more hope to mankind than the promise of an afterlife, with tidings far more interesting than whatever the person who has received the call is doing. Sometimes the companions of the called take their demotion personally, but they are usually old or have something else wrong with them.

While the cell phone has made it much easier to engage in illicit sex, it has perhaps made it more difficult for women to get married. The sound of a woman engaged in chatter unbroken by any time-out for listening to the other person, or breathing, may strike even the slowest bachelor as an awful warning.

The English designer and artist William Morris urged the public to have nothing in their homes that they did not know to be useful or believe to be beautiful. In the users of cell phones, we have ample opportunity to see how the corollary—Say nothing you do not know to be helpful or believe to be interesting—has been taken to heart.

cemetery *n.* The ideal city, in which every wife, husband, and child is loving and beloved. This feast of felicity at times so angers those from the land of the imperfect living that they disfigure the gravestones and dismember the effigies. It might help if future epitaphs read, with more realism, "Not a bad guy when he was sober."

{cemetery}

chains *n.* Restraints to which most people happily submit, feeling their weight not as a burden but a sign of importance. The chains of matrimony, said one philosopher, are so heavy that it takes two to carry them—and sometimes three.

challenging *adj.* Description of a poorly received book, film, or artwork by its creators, who (in public, at least) meet rejection with gentle pity for the prudish and dim.

In the struggle to keep up with fashion, even one's dinner plate becomes a battleground of ideas. One avantgarde chef says his restaurant offers not only dishes that require rethinking the nature of reality but several that are "quite unchallenging." How wise, considering that some food not only poses a challenge but openly doubts you can meet it. See intimidate.

charity *n.* A means for the established rich to publicize their social standing, for the nouveau riche to acquire some, and for the rest to luxuriate in their benevolence by giving away what they do not need.

As well as benefiting their announced recipients, charities relieve taxpayers of the burden of demanding value for money and non-charity workers, at least on weekdays, of the company of those in whom desire to do the right thing is as intense as the belief that theirs is the one right way to do it.

cheerfulness *n.* Sturdy defense against sorrow and ecstasy.

child *n.* Tiny time bomb. Though parents may regard their children as potential heart surgeons, movie stars, or presidents, entitling them to more interest and indulgence than they could claim on their own merits, they know a reckoning awaits. On reaching maturity, children may decide that what has prevented them from attaining these goals—or being socially adept, solvent, or sane—are their parents. Some parents therefore try to dodge these claims by inundating their children with attention, protection, and privilege, at least prior to the divorce. Others follow the simpler and cheaper method of having as little to do with their children as possible.

{child}

While the extreme self-centeredness of so many of the young may seem little different from that of the psychopath, this applies only to other people's children.

child abuse *n.* Torment of an adult who, if left alone for five minutes with a minor whom he has criticized, risks being accused of having succumbed to an illegal impulse.

childhood *n.* Period when one constructs blinders for viewing the world and records the voice that issues marching orders. "I built my whole life on hating my father," says the title character in Sidney Kingsley's play *Detective Story.* "All the time he was inside me, laughing."

While the happy childhood is generally considered preferable, the unhappy one has much to be said for it. Not only does it increase one's appreciation of the rest of life, it prepares one for the other end, in which contempt and indifference become the fate of far more than those who suffered them at the beginning.

In their second childhood, old people who behave like small children who have not yet learned manners are thought to have forgotten theirs. Perhaps, though, they are raging at the fraud perpetrated so many years ago, when they were told, "Grabbing things and making a fuss will not get you what you want."

choice *n.* (1) Right denied to ailing Europeans, who must accept treatment by any doctor who happens to be available. Defended by Americans, who guard their freedom to die in any gutter they choose. (2) Conscious decision by which one, having weighed the alternatives, embarks upon a life of success or failure, glory or crime. Incorrect ones deserve only sympathy.

cigarette *n.* Weapon of mass destruction, capable of causing permanent lung damage to anyone within fifty yards; its effects are particularly harmful to children, especially if they are cute. After several cigarettes in quick succession, smokers are known to slur their speech, become nasty and aggressive, operate machinery in a dangerous manner, and expel unpleasant bodily substances in public.

{cigarette}

civil union *n.* Form of marriage that sounds superior to the usual kind but may be no more courteous. As Brendan Behan remarked of the conflict in Ireland, "If this is a civil war, I'd hate to see an uncivil one."

clarify *v.* To retrieve an opinion made in haste for editing, such as inserting or removing the word "not." Much in favor among politicians, movie stars, and other dispensers of ethical philosophy.

cleansing *n.* The ritual process of preparing the groom for matrimony, during which he is combed for parasites and other unsanitary friends.

clothing *n.* Articles by which anyone can increase the amount of beauty in the world. Evidently, most people think there is quite enough and more might prove distracting.

cohabitation *n.* Humane process in which a man becomes married by imperceptible degrees, like a lobster whose cooking is started in cold water.

collectible *n.* Object that many are eager to possess, though it may not be attractive, entertaining, or useful. Not to be confused with "spouse."

color *v.* To change the hue of one's hair for reasons of employment, fashion, or psychological health rather than, like those who dye it, deceit. The ancient Greeks took a more forthright view:

> Mycilla dyes her locks, 'tis said,
> But 'tis a foul aspersion.
> She buys them black; they therefore need
> No subsequent immersion.

commitment *n.* Allegiance to opinion, product, or other person, a hindrance to self-realization in this world of infinite opportunities. As commitment may be considered to be made by a careless word, or three, the shrewd take their pleasures with no sign of enjoyment. The forward motion of lust for consumption and self-expression, countered by the backward step of fear of commitment, provides the illusion of stability.

common sense *n.* Oxymoronically named quality considered more than a match for knowledge, sensitivity, and principles. Its most frequent use is to justify the belief that whatever is, is right, at least when the chips fall the speaker's way.

community *n.* Group of several thousand or million people who think and vote the same way, e.g., blacks, gays, Muslims, Jews.

compassion *n.* Enemy of competence.
The Dalai Lama says that compassion is the best response to one's enemies, and that saintly man is right on the money. Approaching your enemies with compassion for the personal inadequacies that have driven them

to unpleasant behavior can often reduce them to quivering wrecks.

complain *v.* To denounce unfairly. A way to discover, in a hotel or restaurant, that self-abnegation is not, despite appearances, extinct. On pointing out the grossest rudeness or incompetence, one will be told, in shock and bewilderment, "No one has ever complained before." Though discourteous in speech, the complaint may be made in writing. A letter to a government or corporation about a serious error, inadequacy, or offense will receive the reassuring response "You have every right to complain."

complete with *adj.* Phrase designating something whose absence would be noticed only by the person owning or selling it.

compliment *n.* Verbal gift, of which it is as unwise as it is unmannerly to ask the price. An author told "You're my favorite writer!" will ask the name of the second favorite only once.

compromise *n.* State in which neither party is satisfied. Far better is conquest, in which one is.

condolence *n.* Balm usually applied in inverse proportion to the severity of the wound. On making a trivial mistake, one risks being slathered with condolence by the sensitive and made to feel that the error is a good deal worse than one thought. The death of a spouse or child, however, often arouses in them only a noble reluctance to blame you for having made them feel awkward.

confession *n.* Act that, in our efficient world, now incorporates contrition, repentance, reparation, and, if a publisher is interested, remuneration.

confidence *n.* Belief in one's character and competence, conferred by one's ignorance and sustained by the ignorance or timidity of others. At times confidence does not occur naturally and blossoms only when grafted from a loving spouse. As such spouses often discover too late, the newly confident may embark on a folie à deux with herself or himself, or with a third party, leaving no passion for the lawful mate.

conscience *n.* Mental anachronism that prevents you from feeling good about yourself.

conservative *adj.* Popular political position, as it appeals to both optimists (the world could not be better) and pessimists (any change is for the worse) and requires no knowledge beyond the title of the Groucho Marx song "Whatever It Is, I'm Against It." In England, the Conservatives are known as "the stupid party." Not always invalid, though it can be misleading, like a stopped clock 1,438 minutes a day.

constituency *n.* Collection of the most deprived and deserving people in the country.

Constitution *n.* American document whose brilliant but high-minded authors envisioned no conflict between liberty and the pursuit of happiness. Often cited by those who believe our ancestors suffered opprobrium, imprisonment, and death so we could shout "Fuck!" in a crowded elevator.

contentment *n.* Un-American condition detrimental to the economy and political ambition, but fortunately rare. Defined by the poet and essayist Randall Jarrell as a state achieved only in retrospect: "The people who live in a Golden Age usually go around complaining how yellow everything looks."

contradiction *n.* Technique affording those with little or no knowledge of a topic the ability to participate in or dominate a conversation. Its frequency and vehemence tend to increase once the speaker decides that he has reached the age at which he has learned all he needs to know. This age can vary by about sixty years.

control *n.* Necessary condition for the emotionally fragile, for whom fortunately there are always plenty of sturdier souls to prevent mental disintegration and to deny the wicked suggestion that the desired state is very like tyranny. "Barbara suffers terribly from her need to always be in control."

controversial *adj.* Way of describing a vile person whose admirers might cancel their subscriptions or a saint whose detractors must be likewise conciliated.

cook *v.* (1) To apply heat to food in order to render it inedible. (2) To bring a meal into being with the aid of various utensils, such as the telephone. (3) To take part, on television, in a spectator sport. The female audience, when it tires of romance novels, turns to cookbooks as escapist entertainment.

It may seem bizarre that so many people heat a dinner that is already prepared and that often looks as if it has already been eaten instead of taking the same time or less to cook a better and cheaper meal at home. The stomach, however, has no chance against the ego, which considers a higher price for worse food good value if it purchases the labor of a servant, however incompetent.

cool *adj.* Of a person, cold.

counterintuitive *adj.* Of a thought that rebelliously and maliciously suggests one might be wrong.

courage *adj.* Obsolete virtue. In its resemblance to denial, an impediment to the smooth functioning of the consumer society.

courtship *n.* Period in which the wording of the contract can be altered, albeit in invisible ink.

credit *n.* Concatenation of innumeracy, insecurity, disinhibition, and lack of regard for the future. Unlike sex without contraception, which can also be so described, it usually permits return or exchange.

cretin *n.* Word derived from "Christian," applied to these unfortunates by the charitable, who wanted them to be called by a name that applied to everyone and ended up making their point in a slightly different way. Also, a cross borne by the inhabitants of Crete, whose name is a homonym, as many tourists discover each year, when they can be sure, perhaps for the only time, that the word does not apply to them.

critic *n.* Writer whose unfavorable opinion of someone's work is a personal attack on its creator or an excuse to indulge his bad qualities—when you ask critics to understand, said Hemingway, "they bring envy and jealousy." When asked, "What gives you the right to be a critic?" the impertinent author never shows a license, diploma from critic school, or other reasonable qualification. He may sometimes brood that members of far more demanding occupations, such as doctors, are always assumed to be as qualified for their jobs as the critic is not for his, though no critic ever cut off someone's good leg.

Those whose amour propre has been wounded by critics should remember that these poor creatures are all too conscious of their ineffectiveness. Once in a great while, a critic may make an obscure work into a mild success or laugh a terrible show out of business, but real critics have never had anything like the sensational effect of the fictional ones in William March's novel *The Bad Seed*. On asking a book group how to end a novel in which a woman discovers her little daughter is a serial killer, the presumed author is told that the woman should kill the girl, then herself. The "author" goes home and follows their advice, for she is the mother of this evil child. Of such a tribute to his judgment, the critic can only dream.

cryptamnesia *n.* Belief that one is thinking or feeling something for the first time when in fact one is only remembering it. Defense of plagiarists, balm for lovers, necessity for artists.

culture *n.* (1) Any activity that, because done by a group of people for a long time, deserves to be taken seriously—e.g., "gang culture," "drinking culture," and, as one newspaper reported of the statutory rape long practiced on Pitcairn Island, "a culture of child abuse." The author once applied to be a mentor of poor children and was warmly received. When asked for their suggestions on getting the children to stop swearing, however, the welcoming committee fell silent. "I wouldn't dream of telling them to stop swearing," said a stunned charity worker. "Of course not," said another. "That's their culture." (2) A divisive force that, added to money, produces social class.

curiosity *n.* Belief that people or subjects everyone does not know or events everyone has not witnessed might be interesting, a sign in some circles that one is worryingly radical or extremely ill mannered. On some occasions, however, it may be permitted, as a novel diversion—e.g., "Now, what exactly is this Internet I've been hearing about? Do you have one? I want you to tell me *all* about it!"

customer *n.* More important person than "passenger," "citizen," or any other description not concerned with money. "Manners will never be universally good," said one economic philosopher, "until every person is every other person's customer."

cutting-edge *adj.* Capable of inflicting pain, a desirable quality often claimed for consumer goods.

cynic *n.* A romantic with the fur side inside.

{cynic}

damn *v.* Curse rendered obsolete by more forceful alternatives and declining concern about the section of the afterlife in which one ends up. With sex, shopping, and the Internet absent from the supposedly preferable place, they now seem much the same.

dating *v.* Fucking. Though reading about, watching, or even performing coition is the nation's second- or third-favorite activity, and the verb is used freely to strangers, it is immodest to say that one does it and at times actionable to say that others do. Catherine Deneuve had a daughter, a newspaper reported, "after dating Marcello Mastroianni"; an advice column printed a letter from a woman who wrote, "I'm happy to go out to dinner with him, but I'm not interested in dating"; and an anti-Clinton crowd greeted the philandering president with the chant "Two, four, six, eight, married people shouldn't date!" The new meaning of the verb allows a woman whose relationship with a man amounted to only a few telephone calls to imply that she merited considerably more trouble and expense, but it is hard on old ladies who can no longer tell their grandchildren that, when young, they were popular and dated lots of men.

death *n.* Event whose unknown arrival time and lack of photo opportunities lead many to doubt it will arrive at all.

denial *n.* Class-dependent response to a charge of wrongdoing. The lower-class person—even when confronted by eyewitnesses, fingerprints, DNA deposits, and CCTV footage—maintains, "It wasn't me." The middle-class miscreant acknowledges the deed but explains why only the narrow-minded and misguided would condemn it. The upper-class criminal, affronted, declares, "I don't know what you're talking about." One more example of how the upper and lower classes find natural a radical solipsism with which the middle class still struggles.

deserve *v.* Exist.

desperation *n.* Natural condition of human existence. Thoreau wrote that the mass of men live lives of quiet desperation. That of women tends to be the noisy kind.

detox *v.* To use an expensive product to remove from the body all traces of substances not sold by the manufacturer.

developing *adj.* Of a nation once described as "underdeveloped." Those who have not noticed anything to justify the change are overlooking the development of new ways of killing the inhabitants and stealing their aid money.

diary *n.* Record of youthful cruelty and idiocy that, when read decades later, produces in its now normally insensitive author a warm glow at having become wise and kind.

diet *n.* One of the few ways in which Westerners can empathize with the poor of Asia and Africa.

different *adj.* Often redundant, if not erroneous, distinction. "Before meeting her fiancé, the love of her life, she was married to three different men."

dignity *n.* Mental deficit that prevents one from believing that the purchase of a fashionable item or the performance of an absurd sexual act is necessary to one's existence.

diploma *n.* Piece of paper that separates the slow from the imbecile or from imbeciles without money. See academic.

disadvantaged *adj.* Defects of feet, ears, and mouth that render one incapable of walking to a school or library, listening to a policeman, or preventing oneself from threatening strangers, these disabilities to be taken into account by the sentencing judge.

discrimination *n.* (1) The practice of subjecting members of minority groups to mistreatment or deprivation. Destructive to the ideals of democracy. (2) The ability to tell the ugly from the beautiful, the shoddy from the well made, the foolish from the wise. Destructive to the practice of democracy.

disgrace *n.* Marketing opportunity.

disillusion n. Process that converts the peanut butter of romance into the peanuts of matrimony.

dissatisfaction *n.* Reaction on receiving what one has requested or earned. Means of showing that, despite appearances, one is deserving of a great deal more. The quest for satisfaction has become a duty to oneself that often ends only with bankruptcy or senility. "The disappointed," said the British prime minister and novelist Benjamin Disraeli, "are always young."

diversity *n.* Doctrine that variety is the spice of life and the ideal habitat an Indian restaurant. Not followed by the poet Philip Larkin, who—on being reproved for a criticism with "What sort of world would it be if everyone were like you?"—replied, "I think it would be *wonderful.*"

Though diversity is promoted by apparent liberals (the true liberal being generous, not mindless), its philosophy was expressed first and most forcefully by a conservative, Senator Roman Hruska. In 1970, defending a Supreme Court nominee who had been called a mediocrity, he argued, "There are a lot of mediocre judges and people and lawyers. They are entitled to a little representation, aren't they?" At the time he was ridiculed and his candidate defeated. Time, however, has proved him a visionary.

divorce *n.* The secular version of being born again, when one is washed in the blood of attorney's fees and sees the light that the faults in one's marriage were the other party's.

doctorate *n.* Certificate entitling the holder to be called "doctor" but likely to be so addressed only by a German or the person in the mirror. Guarantee of respect from maître d's, though likely to be withdrawn if another diner has a heart attack.

dog *n.* The last innocent in a wicked world. "What is the difference between a dog and a man?" asked Mark Twain. "If you take a starving dog home and feed him, he will not bite you." Unable to dissimulate, ever optimistic and loving, and dependent on a human sense of responsibility for his food and evacuations, the dog is increasingly unsuited

{dog}

for contemporary society. The cat, on the other hand, which buries its indiscretions, reserves commitment, and is skilled at inducing inferiority and guilt, is superlatively adapted to it. For this reason, cats make excellent marriages and head many of the major corporations.

domination *n.* Iron glove that, in a marriage of equals, both spouses take turns wearing.

dried plum *n.* It's a prune. Grow up.

dumbing down *n.* Dopey phrase condemning stupidity. Popular with those who, wishing to publicize their high standards, sound as if they have never used any slang and are now, in their bravado, getting it wrong.

earn *v.* Show up.

earthy *adj.* Way to describe a joke or person to someone who might be put off by a display of taste or morality.

eccentric *n.* One who is oddly dressed, ill mannered, and rich.

ecology *n.* Concern of political groups and charities devoted to the preservation or improvement of natural phenomena, which, unlike poor people, cannot impugn the motives and methods of their patrons.

edit *v.* To remove from a book, article, or television program anything that, even if advancing readers' or viewers' knowledge, might cause them to become angry or confused. The standard for intellect and open-mindedness is the editor, who is often heard to say, "Of course I understand it, but they won't." There is a saying in newspaper offices that you cannot print anything so bad it will not cause a reader to tell you it changed his life or so great that it will not make him cancel his subscription.

education *n.* Process that, in apprising one of the world's riches, creates a painful feeling of deprivation, and, of the injustice of the world, a perpetual fever of resentment. Discouraged, therefore, by responsible parents.

Just as the earlier onset of menstruation (see menarche) has paralleled increased encouragement of sexual activity, the standards of public education have become steadily lower as the demand for uneducated workers has decreased. This is called government planning.

ego *n.* That which renders us incapable of making a noise to annoy ourselves or being disgusted by anything we say, no matter how much revulsion the same words would cause us from someone else.

elitism *n.* Granting of respect or influence, in some countries, to people with money and powerful ancestors; in others, people of intelligence and talent. Both systems are regarded in America as reactionary and not very nice.

e-mail *n.* Technological advance that ensures that one's letter will not be ignored by a correspondent too busy to write a reply, find a stamp, and walk to a mailbox. Instead, one's message is sent to a person too busy to type two words and click.

empower *v.* (1) To enable to make a purchase or create a nuisance. (2) To instill false hope: "The children were empowered by the increase in their self-esteem." (3) To give a sum or service that contributes far less to the recipient than to the donor's self-satisfaction. Seen on the envelope of a charity that had been given free postage: "Empowered by Pitney Bowes."

England *n.* Country where everyone is a butler or has one and all speak in a way that proclaims their superiority either with bell-like clarity or mesmerizing unintelligibility.

Enlightenment *n.* Intellectual revolution of eighteenth-century Europe, in support of reason and liberty, which has not yet reached many Asian and African countries, as is often noted by those who deplore their ignorance, corruption, and cruelty. The prevalence of these evils in countries that have known the principles of the Enlightenment for three hundred years is more difficult to explain and will require many millions of dollars in research grants.

enthusiasm *n.* Lack of interest.

equality *n.* State marked by perpetual striving for the role of *primus inter pares.*

essential *adj.* Supererogatory.

ethical *adj.* Explanation of higher price.

etiquette *n.* Socially approved behavior that, though irksome to many, promotes the happiness of all—e.g., thank-you notes for gifts, black at funerals, sex on the third date.

euphemism *n.* Emollient synonym that spares the feelings of the speaker. The man who passes the physically challenged homeless man without enabling his feelings of dependency does so in a better frame of mind than the man who stiffs the cripple.

evil *adj.* Term used in less enlightened societies to denounce people we now know will respond well to sympathetic listening and fresh fruit.

excellence *n.* Word once inferred, now, in a world that encourages diversity, considered a necessary clarification. One institution claims that it is "devoted to teaching excellence in leadership."

exclusive *adj.* (1) Of an object, the promise that the joy of possessing it will be enhanced by contemplating the misery of those denied it. A seductive claim, even if everyone knows it means only "expensive." (2) Of a relationship, one free from rivals, even if the likelihood of any is notional or ridiculous. Also expensive.

experience *n.* The best teacher, in charge of a class busy sending text messages.

expert *n.* Member of a revered minority who, while unable to solve your problem, can tell you why everyone who disagrees with him is wrong. The expert witness is one whose knowledge is so broad as to include support for the view of whoever is paying him. Those with broad knowledge of experts tend to believe their opinion is frequently no better than that of any observant person with a reasonable amount of logic, detachment, and experience—but that is, of course, merely to switch from one small minority to another.

explain *v.* To give reasons for the correctness of one's point of view so the other party may avoid embarrassment or bloodshed. Ring Lardner writes in a short story about a man silencing his offspring: "'Shut up,' he explained."

Facebook *n.* Website patronized by those who believe their faces an encouragement to further acquaintance.

face-lift *n.* Surgical procedure that, in making a few, hardly noticeable alterations to a woman's face, leaves it fixed in incredulity at the vanity of others.

fact *n.* Ineffectual support for argument. "Don't bother me with details," the person knowing many facts will be told by one taking the opposite view. "I'm talking about principles."

failure *n.* Everybody. We have all done things we ought not to have done and failed to do things we should have done. The inveterate failure is summed up in the Yiddish proverb "If he sold shrouds, people would stop dying."

fairness *n.* Quality that gives niceness a higher value than knowledge. Advocates of fairness often favor the temporal means of determining who has facts or morals on his side: "You had your way last week/year/war, so let him have his way now."

It is sometimes conceded of a criticism that it is "harsh but fair." The mild-but-fair criticism has yet to be made.

{face-lift}

false volition *n.* Popular sentence construction of a narcissistic age: "I had my pocket picked yesterday." "I had my nose broken in the accident." Avoids the onerous mental effort needed to cast a sentence in the passive voice and allows the speaker to sound in command of the situation, which is more important than sounding masochistic or insane.

family *n.* Group in which some exercise power without skill or justice and others bide their time, taking notes.

family name *n.* Term identifying related people, once preceded in direct address by Miss, Mrs., or Mr. to show respect, but now, with the decline in the influence—indeed, existence—of the family, seldom used. The sense of inferiority implied by the notion that another automatically deserves respect is now found insulting; the sense of responsibility implied by being so addressed is considered frightening.

famous *adj.* Of a person, place, thing, or event that you cannot count on those you are addressing to know.

fanatic *n.* Believer.

fantasy *n.* Temporary belief in the impossible that, depending on time, place, and degree of indulgence, can indicate harmless time-wasting or mental disturbance. A boy who each day talks to an imaginary friend may well worry a mother who does so only once a week.

fashion *n.* Influence that the wise know is responsible for what we think, feel, say, and do and that fools believe tells us only what to wear.

fast food *n.* Edible matter that shortens the time necessary to reach the grave.

fat *n.* Result of understandable desire to put as much space as possible between oneself and other people.

fatherhood *n.* Complicity between men to create a supply of young, acquiescent second wives. The father's remoteness from his daughter ensures that she will grow up eager to serve and adore a man, even one of negligible fiscal or moral worth, who is at least twenty years older and pays her some attention.

fault *n.* In a purchased object, a defect that spurs demands for instant repair or replacement and compensation for mental or physical distress. In oneself, an intrinsic and unchangeable personality trait responsible for much of one's charm. Awareness, much less criticism, of a fault by a teacher, partner, colleague, or spouse is an alarm that tells us the other person is disloyal and perhaps dangerous. Preemptive violence, desertion, or a charge of sexual harassment is a wise move.

In theory, it is not necessary to expunge all faults from one's character. One need only know oneself well enough to refrain from manifesting them too often, or at least to apologize afterward. One's spouse can help by saying, with a friendly smile, "Dear, you're doing that thing again." Some spouses are optimistic enough to try this twice.

feelings *n.* Mental bowel movements productive of truth and prognostication. Once expressed in private to one's intimates, now exhibited in public to all, who will, if they have any decency, understand.

Like other people's religion, parents, and children, other people's feelings are sacred, especially those of the young. At one high school, an English teacher who wanted to distribute a list of great books that pupils should have read before they left was fortunately stopped just in time. Teenagers who were about to graduate or had already done so might see that they had not read most of the books, she was told, and their feelings would be hurt.

One school of thought holds that it is not possible to restrain or disguise one's feelings. Many of this persuasion, however, also believe that it is possible for another person to love them without being aware of it.

Not long ago there was a fashion in books that instructed women how to talk to men about feelings. The theory was that men were not really cold and selfish—they just didn't understand how their behavior made women feel. The men would change, it was promised, once it was explained to them, slowly, in words they could understand, the distress that nastiness and selfishness caused their girl-friends or wives. The wounds caused by this disregard of the excellent maxim "Even if it's broke, don't fix it" have not yet healed.

Those who hold that feelings prompted by the heart are so insistent that they must be appeased should perhaps consider the appearance of those who believe the same of feelings emanating from the stomach.

feminism *n.* Social movement that has freed women to take any job that will enable them, together with their mates, to keep a roof over their heads and send their children to a decent private school. The cost of housing may or may not reflect the tendency of banks, as a result of feminist campaigning, to take a wife's earnings into account in determining mortgage eligibility, just as the decline of public schools may or may not result from the freedom women now have to take more rewarding jobs than teaching.

Feminists can be men as well as women. The male feminist abhors the idea of a spouse who submits to him in public and in private; the latter is, for him, quite sufficient.

Though some men reflexively deride feminists as ugly, ugly women are as likely to be antifeminist, at least when men are around, as the pretty and stupid: It is their only form of coquetry. Unfortunately, they forget that sycophancy is a coin whose value depends on the hand that gives it. No Hollywood producer ever surrounded himself, at least in the boardroom, with yes-women.

femme fatale *n.* Woman whose allure owes much to a corpse-like lack of animation that men consider a challenge and to a deadly lack of humor that guarantees she will never find them a source of comedy.

fidelity *n.* Principle that keeps spouses loyal to each other while occupying the same room.

{fidelity}

fire *n.* Early technological development, perhaps a mistake, as it has turned out to have, along with its benefits, many unpleasant applications.

first *adv., adj.* Qualifier often attached to "began" or "started" to indicate the earliest of the many beginnings possible now that one can efface the past. (See reinvent.)

A first, or starter, marriage is now widely recognized as a proving ground for a later, more advanced model. "One's so busy learning how to be married at all," wrote the novelist Anthony Berkeley, "that one can hardly help acquiring a kind of resentment against one's partner in error."

flattery *n.* Acknowledgment of virtues that others are too dim to see or too envious to praise. "He who says he hates every kind of flattery," said the philosopher Georg Christoph Lichtenberg, "does not yet know every kind of flattery."

fool *n.* Some of the people all the time and all the people some of the time. The likelihood of being one or being with one is often in inverse ratio to one's certainty that this is not the case. In *The Matchmaker,* by Thornton Wilder, a character declares that "99 percent of people are fools, and the rest of us are in danger of contagion." As the title character points out, however, quarantine is no protection, so one's only choice is whether to be "a fool among fools or a fool alone."

foreigner *n.* One whose English, learned in his own country, is superior to that of native speakers but, deficient in slang and obscenity, may be ridiculed for its inauthenticity.

forever *adv.* Till something better comes along. The hyperbole of lovers' promises has seeped into journalism, whose practitioners write, "His book forever changed the way we think about the subject" and "The journey changed their lives forever," secure in the belief that, with their own passing, not only the world but time will end.

forgive *v.* Infuriate. Where refusal to forgive is more wounding, this, of course, should be practiced, but in the long run it is usually less effective, as well as less satisfying, since graciousness gets better publicity. As a misbehaving character in a Graham Greene novel is sweetly pardoned by his wife, "the word 'forgive' tolled on in William's ears like the bell at Newgate signaling an execution."

formal *adj.* Pertaining to an activity that requires a clean T-shirt.

Fortune *n.* Churlish goddess whose gifts, however many, suggest the many more she refuses to bestow.

freedom *n.* Condition demanded by the young until they realize how troublesome and confusing it is, and better left to experts, such as the rich.

free time *n.* Commodity too precious to be spent on activities that do not cost money.

friend *n.* One whose self-delusions we leave intact in exchange for reciprocal courtesy, and whose vices, being the same as ours, do not annoy us. As this suggests, friendship involves a rationality and objectivity often lacking in sexual relations. E. M. Forster's declaration that he would sooner betray his country than his friend lost a lot of its nobility when it became clear that the latter was a euphemism.

{formal}

frigidity *n.* A charge whose validity sometimes turns on whether the man making it and its object have shared a bed.

fulfillment *n.* Nirvana that awaits one who has gratified society and, incidentally, himself by making the best use of his myriad talents. Justification for bad debts, promiscuity, and divorce.

funeral *n.* Opportunity, like weddings and christenings, for social climbing. On the death of Diana, princess of Wales, John Travolta announced that he was available to comfort her sons.

gallant *adj.* A compliment or favor, when there is no hope of reward, is considered gallant. A gallant man, however, may not have considered that being fat, married, or forty years older than the one he flatters could be an impediment to romance. The lady in question often receives the gesture with a sickly smile, knowing that it means she is being enrolled in his fantasies.

G
H

garden *n.* Residential plot, once the imperfect product of time, effort, and subjection to nature, now, like food and sex, obtainable quickly and in superior form with a telephone call.

generalization *n.* Partial truth, claimed to be wholly untrue if it threatens anyone's vanity or finances. Meant to be suggestive rather than conclusive, the generalization, indispensable for theory and strategy, is often hotly disputed by those who consider neither so important as sanctimony.

genitalia *n.* Judging by advertising, entertainment, and human behavior, the parts of one's own body considered most important. Judging by the use of their demotic names to or about others, terms of extreme contempt.

genius *n.* Faculty said by Thomas Edison to be composed of 1 percent inspiration and 99 percent perspiration, a belief responsible for all those publicly displayed buckets of sweat.

gentleman *n.* Man who, if priding himself on being one, does not answer the description. The "gentleman of the old school," whose only attainment is what he regards as his exquisite manners, expects a woman, in return for holding her coat and the door, to regard him as a god and herself as his slave. "We received a visit from the father of M. d'Aux, a gentleman of the old school, without a vestige of intelligence or learning. It used to be said of him that he had, quite literally, bored his wife to death" (*Memoirs,* Madame de La Tour du Pin).

gesture *n.* Increasingly frequent aid to speech that, in our inarticulate time, has added a note of Mediterranean gaiety to previously undemonstrative Anglo-Saxon countries—until one notices that the accompanying smiles are sheepish or desperate.

good *adj.* (1) In some cases, bad. If the adjective is used when it should go without saying, one should not rely on the judgment of the speaker. Someone who loves good food can be found tucking into an econo-size mystery burger. A person described as having a good sense of humor will not get the point of remarks made by someone with a sense of humor. (2) Virtuous in a way that profits no one. A good woman was once understood to be kind, charitable, or chaste. The virtuous woman of our own time refuses whole milk, fried potatoes, and the slice of pie, then exercises by hugging herself as she proclaims, "I'm so *good!*"

government *n.* Administrative entity made up of people without the talent to go into business for themselves—with, of course, some exceptions, as enterprising reporters sometimes discover. When a problem is called to its attention, a government typically appoints a committee to conduct an investigation and issue a report that concludes that the best policy, all things considered, would be to wait and see. The legislators spring into action, however, when confronted with a problem that demands urgent resolution, such as the finding that members of the government are not being paid enough.

grumpy *adj.* Annoyed by such trifles as illiteracy, illegitimacy, drunkenness, and drug addiction. The tedious and risible grumpiness of the old is quite different from the emotion of the young who denounce smoking, failure to recycle, and the unwillingness of their families to give them money. That is principled indignation.

guilt *n.* (1) Feeling that discourages self-indulgence. Though conducive to the material well-being of psychoanalysts, its dampening effect on the happiness and profit of most others accounts for its declining popularity. (2) Substitute for reform or reparation, unfortunately not in currency recognized by creditors. (3) Cause of distress to and reason for sympathy with the wrongdoer.

gun *n.* Means by which the inarticulate can settle disputes and the shy can ensure attention. A democracy always has to find some means of balancing the advantages of the clever and bold. The expectation, by gun carriers, that they may be threatened with murder at any time is not at odds with traditional American optimism: What could be better than starring in your own Western?

{gun, handbag}

handbag *n.* Carrier for the impedimenta of a woman's face and identity. The small handbag is favored by some as conveying the idea that its owner, like the queen of England, does not need to work. The large handbag, however, is generally preferred, as it can cost as much as five automobiles, a more emphatic indication of wealth than the small handbag, which can cost only the same as one.

While, a few decades ago, most women would own a single black handbag for a long time, they are now likely to have several bags, some brightly colored and frivolous, that they discard when they tire of them. In the same period, women's sexual partners have increased in number, variety, and publicity. Despite Freud's identification of the symbolism of the handbag, this is a coincidence.

handpicked *adj.* Superior to that chosen by the foot.

hanging out *v.* Like "chilling," a term that suggests the inarticulate and idle are engaged in some definite, even sophisticated, activity.

happiness *n.* A state rarely achieved by both members of a couple at the same time, and then, as at least one of them usually recalls afterward, only with a degree of self-deception. The desire for happiness—portrayed as the only alternative to despondency—is the postindustrial society's motivation for perpetual consumption, but the object of that desire is for many people unattainable. "Actual happiness," said Aldous Huxley, "always looks pretty squalid in comparison with the over-compensations for misery."

If, however, happiness itself is beyond one's reach, the appearance of happiness should be cultivated if only for the rage it inspires in others.

hat *n.* Item of attire whose obsolescence is responsible for the collapse of Western manners. In its last days, the American hatters' association announced that a hat was indispensable because, without one to raise, a man had no way of acknowledging a woman.

The man considered most responsible for the hat's demise is John F. Kennedy. He did, however, have his own way.

{hat}

heart *n.* Popular euphemism for hormones.

he/she *pron.* When addressing his or her companion, the correct way of referring to the person in the wheelchair.

high-minded *adj.* With the head at an altitude where oxygen cannot reach the brain.

historical novel *n.* Work of fiction in which authors with no idea of how people think, speak, and behave in the present describe how they thought, spoke, and behaved in the past.

history *n.* Discipline that, in reminding us that the world existed before we did, creates identity malfunction and is therefore banned from schools along with foreign languages, the province of obstinate and eccentric foreigners.

Those who worry that, if we do not study history, we are doomed to repeat it need not be concerned. Everyone, whether or not he studies history, is doomed to repeat history.

hobby *n.* Pastime allowing one to express a greater range of tastelessness and incompetence than is possible in one's occupation and home life.

Holocaust *n.* Event whose survivors have caused so much irritation with their cry of "Never again!" that others have understandably said that it never existed, that it was much exaggerated, that the victims brought it upon themselves, or that the survivors' children have repeated it. Nobody likes to be nagged.

homeopathy *n.* Like sympathy and empathy, a way of curing disease.

home-wrecker *n.* Husband-stealer—far less wicked, in women's eyes, than one who steals a lover.

Homo sapiens *n.* Taxonomists' joke.

homosexual *n.* Male who derives pleasure from relations with other males, as distinct from a heterosexual man, who derives pleasure from the envy or fellow feeling that his relations with females inspire in other men. Often angers the married man by his indifference to a status purchased at great emotional, physical, and financial sacrifice to ensure social acceptance and the regular provision of clean shirts and socks.

As cannot be stated often enough, education is the way to overcome prejudice. Once everyone learned that gay men possess a high degree of disposable income, opposition to them melted away.

honesty *n.* Crude attempt at persuasion practiced by those who lack wealth, beauty, or social standing.

honorable *adj.* Characteristic of one who, when bought, stays bought.

hospital *n.* Social club for diseases.

humility *n.* Attitude required for the acquisition of knowledge. Often considered more irksome than remaining ignorant, as it may blemish one's self-esteem. Though humility may seem unpleasant to one who tries it with a finger or toe, total immersion may prove unexpectedly refreshing. The author was quite heartened when, on asking a Catholic friend for advice on a question that, if decided wrongly, could ruin her life, he thought about it and replied, "Would that matter?"

Hygeia *n.* Goddess worshipped by most Americans. Her temple can be recognized by the odors of its incense, disinfectant, and air freshener, the last named by someone with a sense of humor. Her devotees have been known to perform their rites with such zeal that their children can grow up without making the acquaintance of a bacterium and lack immunity to later exposure. Pharmaceutical companies, however, can provide more products to remedy the problems the first lot caused.

hyphen *n.* Punctuation used in the self-description of many in the land where all are equal but some like to hedge their bets.

hypocrisy *n.* Mythical vice. Accusations of hypocrisy are made by the ignorant and vindictive, who do not know or pretend not to know the precise circumstances that render the charge invalid.

Though the hypocrite may annoy, he has his uses. If you are assaulted in view of people you know, the arm-chair warrior or the wife-beating humanitarian will feel a greater obligation to help than the plain-speaking coward or misanthrope.

iconic *adj.* Of a person, object, or incorporeal entity ("It was an iconic moment in sports when . . .") guaranteed reverence in the universal religions of fame and money.

iconoclast *n.* One who smashes the clay and wooden idols within easy reach and does not strain himself or credulity by breaking those made of silver and gold.

idealist *n.* One who harms another only regretfully and for a very good reason. His victims, accidental or intentional, are enjoined to take the long view.

A purist, the idealist does not love people but qualities. People, while tolerable as vessels for them, are resented for also containing lesser qualities, like a rich, lovely bride with coarse relatives.

identify *v.* To decide that another person's character, mentality, or experiences are identical to one's own, thereby conferring on him or her importance or, indeed, reality. The sensitive identify with foreigners, the very sensitive with nonhuman species, and the extremely sensitive, such as the author Edna O'Brien, with inanimate objects. The description of a rape in one of her novels originated, she said, from a "childhood memory of the sweeper's brush poking into her family's sooty chimney. 'Yes, yes!' she cried. 'I identified with that chimney!'"

"I don't know" *n.* Former, freely given confession of ignorance, now, with the rise in educational standards, unbearably humiliating. Courtesy now requires the person seeking information, even in cases of imminent danger to life and property, to be patient and sympathetic while the other uses various techniques to disguise his lack of omniscience. These include speaking very slowly, pausing several times, frowning, humming in a sagacious manner, and extending the usual response ("I'm not sure") with "actually," "exactly," "just off the top of my head," or "at this moment in time."

There is an English variant: On occasion the person questioned answers, "I haven't a clue." This may be said in a careless tone, indicating that the information sought is of no importance, or a disdainful one, indicating that the question would be asked only by an idiot or pervert.

Writers who know nothing of a subject but see that as no reason to shut up about it have another option. See arguably.

if *conj.* Modifier used by those who don't want to risk apologizing for nothing. "We are sorry if you have suffered any inconvenience." "I am sorry if I have caused distress by not waiting to publish my account of his sexual habits until after the funeral."

ignorance *n.* Delightful attribute, assuring others that they will be able to shine. The ignorant usually attribute it to circumstance, modestly concealing the great and constant effort they have made to preserve it. Unlike the many other means used to retain the appearance of youth, it costs nothing.

In conversation, the polite ignoramus will, on hearing a fact or explanation, acknowledge the speaker's superiority by interrupting him with "I never knew that!" The extremely well mannered will repeat the exclamation a few seconds or minutes later, sometimes several times, each time emphasizing a different word, and adding, "I always thought it meant _____!" Some consider these remarks self-important or sycophantic, allowable only to husband-hunting young women. In the era of the face-lift, however, many other women need to justify their look of perpetual astonishment.

imagination *n.* Quality that enables us to appreciate the consequences of our actions and the suffering of others. To be discouraged at all costs, as its exercise would paralyze all business and much entertainment.

impartial *adj.* Favoring whoever can pay the highest price or work for the lowest one, no matter what his origins or competence.

impatience *n.* Irritation with the stupid for their stubborn refusal to become intelligent, even for a few minutes.

inappropriate *adj.* Criticism replacing others now deemed damaging to the offender's self-esteem, likely to make the critic feel judgmental, and difficult to spell.

Though "inappropriate" is hugely popular, its antonym is for some reason not widely used as a mark of approval, though there are occasional stabs at it. In her memoir of the disgraced financier Bernard Madoff, his mistress praises his lovemaking as "appropriate."

inarticulate *adj.* Empty-headed. If a speaker or writer cannot tell us his meaning, how can he imagine it in the first place? The same with "visionary" or "experimental" artists who are said to lack the technique to realize their imaginings. "When we say an artist's technique is faulty," wrote the artist Patrick Hughes, "we are giving him the benefit of the doubt to a quite unwarranted degree. . . . No one has a vision in excess of his power to materialize that vision." The last remark of course does not apply to social work and may invalidate the preceding ones for those who believe it shares with art the aim of making people feel better.

inclusive *adj.* Of a strategy that enables an organization to congratulate itself for its willingness to make money.

incredible *adj.* Believable by anyone with the slightest awareness of history, technology, folly, or venality. When used to mean "exciting," "abundant," or the like, it expresses a demand from the inarticulate, even if unknown, for credulity.

Independence Day *n.* Date on which residents of a country celebrate their self-determination with fireworks made in the one to which they have lost their jobs.

{Independence Day}

independent *adj.* Of a person, someone who cannot stand to have other people do things for him or her, a preference often made easy by being someone no one else can stand to have around. Of opinions, those shared with people admired for their independence.

indignation *n.* To the lower class, a demonstration of foolishness; to the middle class, a demonstration of principle; to the upper class, a demonstration of failure.

inexorably *adv.* A five-syllable word that, when combined with "drawn," has a stateliness guaranteeing more sympathy than the bald "I couldn't help it."

inextricably *adv.* The degree, according to journalists, to which items or ideas are linked and that a moment's thought would snap apart.

infallibility *n.* Quality on which the timid and sententious pride themselves. Possessed by the pope and most other men, especially when challenged by a woman. The man who is always right, said Max Beerbohm, is never as right as the man who is sometimes wrong.

infamy *n.* (obsolete) Fame.

ingratitude *n.* Failure to honor a forged contract.

inherited *n.* Of a child's characteristic that is identical with one belonging to a wealthy relative.

inhumanity *n.* Identifying trait of humans.

inimitable *adj.* Of a trait or style so distinctive it can be easily imitated.

innocence *n.* A state, intended by nature to be temporary, artificially preserved by parents and teachers for the convenience of governments and corporations. As the smooth running of society entails a certain degree of cruelty and injustice, and since this requires not only evil participants but indifferent observers, innocence must be maintained, as Edith Wharton put it, to seal "the mind against imagination and the heart against experience." Hence such innocent questions as "But what did the Jews do to make themselves so disliked? They must have done *something*."

innovation *n.* Something that can fail in a new way.

insane *n.* A group the nominally normal regard uneasily, wondering if their lack of sense and grace at all resembles the way they themselves appear to others.

The insane are incarcerated far less often than in the past, society being far more considerate now than formerly. Now that numerous other people shout or swear at invisible persons in public, the insane blend in and are tactfully ignored.

inspiration *n.* The divine fire, which springs up unexpectedly when the Creativity Fairy flicks the switch of her lighter, and is forever denied to those unfortunates whose address she has misplaced. A great author was asked if he wrote every day or only when he was inspired. He said, "The latter. But, you know, it's a funny thing—I sit down at my desk at 8:00 a.m. every day, and, it's quite a coincidence, but, at 8:05 every day, I get inspired."

insurer *n.* Only mourner whose statement that you died too soon can never be impugned for insincerity. If the insurer is the most despondent person at the funeral, the most surprised is often the deceased, who believed himself about to collect the big payout for all those premiums of reluctant virtue.

intelligence *n.* Quality even the most distinguished men disdain in women who have a lot and are awestruck by in women who have a little, judiciously applied. John Stuart Mill, who as a child could simultaneously write Latin with one hand and Greek with the other, was played upon by his future wife as if he were a stringed instrument. "As she had the art of returning his own thoughts to himself, clothed in her own words," said a friend of the groom, "he thought them hers, and wondered at her powers of mind, and the accuracy of her conclusions."

intelligent design *n.* Theory that the nature of the world is, ipso facto, proof of the genius of its creator. Promulgated, oddly, by believers.

intention *n.* Thought without which no action is considered criminal, as in "It was not my client's intention, when he poured gasoline on his wife and lit it, to kill her." One of the many advantages of stupidity.

The ostensibly good intention is often sufficient for its holder to receive credit. Those suggesting that actions, properly performed, are what matter, or that the good intention may not be inspired by altruism but by the desire for power or publicity, are unsuited for polite society.

international law *n.* A body of jurisprudence whose creators live on dry land but whose enforcers dwell in thin air.

Internet *n.* Means of communication that enables us to deal with people without seeing them or speaking to them. To those who believe this undesirable, the Internet provides its own corrective.

intimacy *n.* Propinquity plus mutual misunderstanding.

intimidate *v.* To arouse fear or feelings of unworthiness, an ability once restricted to the rich, strong, or brilliant, now possessed, in a nervous age, by all men, women, and children as well as many vegetables. Not knowing how to cook a type of squash, one man told the *New York Times* that he was "intimidated by zucchini."

intransigence *n.* Self-respect.

invention *n.* Development in transportation, production, or communication that gives new scope to depravity, cruelty, and greed.

investment *n.* Home, artwork, or item of clothing that you cannot afford, whose purchase is urged by the clairvoyant as a certain means of reaping a profit in the future. See unfashionable.

Iowa *n.* Land that, like Brigadoon, emerges from the mists every four years, to provide entrails and other offal in which many believe the name of the next president may be read. Inhabitants who from time to time venture from it have great difficulty convincing others that it exists at all.

The tale is told of one who went to live in New York City and wanted to improve his speech. His elocution teacher asked where he came from, then said, "Now, that's just the sort of thing you want to watch. Here it is pronounced o-HI-o."

irony *n.* Characteristic greatly prized by the English for the feeling of superiority it confers over Americans and anyone else who succeeds in business.

The young and the politic enjoy irony for the freedom it confers of claiming one opinion or its opposite, as convenient. Sophisticated teenage boys like to say, when caught looking at nude photos, that they are ironically contemplating the absurdity or inhumanity of the sex industry. Which will sound plausible when somebody invents ironic masturbation.

irrational *adj.* Normal. It is irrational, says a character in a play by Joe Orton, to expect rationality in an irrational world. Perhaps because he is considered an absurdist, this always gets a big laugh.

irreverence *n.* Quality boasted of by one who tweaks the nose of a hero's statue.

issue *n.* (1) Child. (2) Problem, so called by a person too childish to acknowledge a flaw or accept responsibility for a mistake.

Italy *n.* Country demonstrating, as most women know, that sex appeal, a lovely voice, delicious food, and flattering clothes will absolve one of any amount of cruelty or crime.

jealousy *n.* Reason for most criticism, as in "You're just jealous." The others are ignorance ("What do you know?") or idleness ("Don't you have anything better to do?").

Jesuit *n.* Man. If a married man who has had coitus with a woman not his wife on the kitchen table is asked, "Did you go to bed with her?" he will answer, "No" and be able to pass a polygraph test. He will also pass if asked, "Did you sleep with her?" He answers, "No," having kept his eyes open all night.

joke *n.* Occasionally humorous line or anecdote created by one and repeated by another, who expects as much praise as if it were his own from people whom he is showing that a remark by an absent, unknown person is more interesting than any of theirs.

Many topics formerly thought hilarious are no longer funny on any but the lowest social level. The drunk joke has fallen flat since we discovered feelings, and the mother-in-law joke, once a brotherly expression of universal misfortune, now sounds like the special pleading of a man so inept or impoverished that he cannot win her respect, or so touchy that he cares.

{Jesuit}

judgmental *adj.* View that someone, somewhere, at some time has ever done anything for which he should be criticized. Disapproved of by those who make the judgment that this is wrong.

jury *n.* Twelve people who arouse terror in the defendant who realizes that he may indeed be tried by his peers.

kiss *n.* Expression of passion, affection, or goodwill, sincere or feigned. As the handshake arose from the wish to show that one held no weapon, so the fashion of greeting everyone but the mailman with a kiss may be a means of demonstrating that one's mouth does not hold wicked words. An observant man once said, however, that two women kissing cheeks on meeting bear a distinct resemblance to prizefighters shaking hands.

knave *n.* One who incurs more censure than a fool for an identical act. An example of the prejudice against decisiveness and competence.

K
L

knife *n.* Type of cutlery perplexing to many children, who eventually conclude that its proper use is (as they always say) self-defense.

Know-Nothings *n.* Popular term for the mid-nineteenth-century anti-immigration American Party. The original Know-Nothings were not so called because others were contemptuous of their intellect, but the reason for the name justified anyone who was. At first a secret society, the party told members questioned about their activities to say, "I know nothing." It could not have taken long for

{kiss}

someone who got the same three-word answer from everyone he asked to realize something was up.

"Know thyself" *n.* Advice tendered by the ancient Greeks, regarded as superfluous by the young. Also regarded as superfluous by the middle-aged and the old, and regarded by many of all ages as disruptive or irrelevant.

As with other ancient Greek practices, this type of introspection can be subversive of much modern morality. Many people would be happier and make other people less unhappy if they did what they wanted, not what they thought they should. Knowing what one wants, however, is, like knowing what one likes, not as simple as it might seem. In Preston Sturges's movie *Sullivan's Travels,* the film-director hero is told that his new picture has died in Pittsburgh. He asks, "What do they know in Pittsburgh?" and is told, "They know what they like." The director then says, "If they knew what they liked, they wouldn't live in Pittsburgh."

Labia *n.* Powerful goddess, worshipped by men in addition to their other, subsidiary religion.

labor-saving *adj.* Of a device that previous generations were told would allow us to complete our work in far less time, freeing the rest of the day for leisure. As the present generation knows, however, such a device enables an employer to save the wages of one or more laborers and enables the remaining ones to do a day's work in a morning so they can do another day's work in the afternoon.

lady *n.* Term of abuse.

landlord *n.* Either a homicidal miser or a generous prince, who, with the conscientious or unsavory tenant, is the clearest illustration of the law that opposites attract.

land of opportunity *n.* Formerly, an America in which a poor immigrant could start, build, and run a business. Now so improved that the French, Arabs, Japanese, Germans, and Dutch can own its major industries without leaving home.

La Rochefoucauld *n.* French philosopher whose best-known maxim, that every human act is motivated by self-interest, provides a useful way to distinguish between the sexes. If talking to someone of unknown gender, quote La Rochefoucauld. If the reaction is "Of course not! That's a terrible way to think!" you are talking to a man; if "Tell me something I don't know," a woman.

The word that La Rochefoucauld left out, of course, is "presumed." That some people thought their behavior would benefit them, though true, often strains credulity to the utmost.

laughter *n.* Unreliable instrument of sycophancy, which can be fatally undercut by spontaneity. A giveaway, on reading in public, of incipient insanity. Useful when wanting to keep the adjoining seat vacant. Humming classical music works, too.

lawyer *n.* One who, in a time of linguistic sloppiness, is distinguished by his meticulous attention to the meaning and nuance of words. A journalist who lost his life's savings after claiming that a company had no evidence that its drugs cured people was told, by the sympathetic opposing counsel, that he would have been all right if he had only written "no *reliable* evidence."

learning experience *n.* (1) Someone else's misfortune. (2) Unpaid labor by which the young learn how to avoid work and curry favor in an office.

learning style *n.* According to the new pedagogy, there are three styles of learning: visual (reading the instructions), aural (asking someone how the thing works), and mechanical (taking it apart). According to a renegade teacher, these translate respectively as bright, average, and slow.

left-wing/right-wing *adj.* Designation that spares one the effort of determining which side is correct.

liberal *adj.* Generous in one's estimation of other people's motives and capacities and the improving powers of other people's money.

liberated *adj.* Sprung from the frying pan.

life *n.* Terminal illness.

like *interj.* Conversational signal used by the young to show they are still in rehearsal and not ready for reviews.

loneliness *n.* (1) The solitude of the unmarried. (2) The solitude of the married.

longevity *n.* Race in which women outrun men, the result of their desire to have the last word.

lottery *n.* Method by which the government rewards the virtuous and helps the deserving by much the same method used in its other operations.

love *n.* (1) Feeling of joy and benevolence provoked by another person, at times so intense that one actually notices him or her. (2) Belief that one has found one's ideal. Evaporates, in recriminations, when the beloved turns out to have been guilty of an elaborate deceit. (3) Recognition—sometimes mutual—of charm, intelligence, kindness, etc. in the other party, though such qualities may have escaped the notice of everyone else on the planet. Gore Vidal: "The rocks in her head match the holes in his." (4) Complimentary close of letter to person one has met twice.

lover *n.* Person who alternates the roles of costar and audience in one's personal playhouse.

loyalty *n.* Former virtue, rendered impractical and obsolete by more exciting products and people coming onto the market, since one's first duty is to one's God-given potential. Sometimes evoked as an ideal, by corporations ("customer loyalty") or their employees. A publisher who told a copy editor of an author's complaint that he had added many mistakes to a book was asked, "Whose side are you on?"

luxury *n.* Necessity.

manners *n.* Artificial, onerous barrier to self-expression, their abandonment a great step forward for democracy and the manufacturers of tranquilizers.

marriage *n.* Three-legged race in which the participants' finishing lines lie in opposite directions.

martial *adj.* Word often written in error for "marital," especially by the married.

massive *adj.* Immaterial, as in "He has massive support from liberal Republicans."

M
N

masturbation *n.* Popular pastime that may be pursued without delay, expense, and representations of affection. Useful to boys for gratifying their competitive urge and to girls for judging the inadequacy of a future husband.

maternal instinct *n.* Lust for losers.

mature *adj.* Sensible, responsible, cowardly. A mature woman stops looking for a man who is rich, handsome, and charming and looks instead for one who is loyal, sensitive to her feelings, and handy around the house.

meek *adj.* Those who, preparing to inherit the earth, treat others like dirt.

menarche *n.* Commencement of the female reign over the subject sex. Its age has, fortunately for manufacturers, lowered over the past century; hence the increased stimulation of and tolerance for the desire for earlier and more frequent copulation. This has had the unfortunate by-product of increased illegitimacy and sexual disease, but no merchandising strategy is perfect.

metempsychosis *n.* Doctrine illustrating the bad luck of the living. The present incarnation of one's soul is always the sorriest in a series of previous lives in which one tempted King Solomon or discovered radium. Its believers' permanent look of aggrieved bewilderment is similar to that of pugs, who in the past were royal favorites and now may command only the patronage of a hairdresser in Mobile.

middle class *n.* Group devoted to education and morality, punished for its hostility to progress.

minimalism *n.* Style that allows the cold and vacuous to appear disciplined and refined. "The conspicuous austerity of minimalism," says a prominent decorator, "is a powerful statement about self." This statement can be made only by those for whom austerity is a choice. The cold and vacuous poor are out of luck.

mirror *n.* Device once found in every home, now too expensive for mass ownership.

miscegenation *n.* Response to increasing androgyny.

misfortune *n.* Insolence of the gods.

misogynist *n.* Desirable man. With some, the condition is the cause of the belief, as he sees women at their most shameless. With others, the reverse applies: Every attractive woman likes a challenge.

mistake *n.* Minor error in judgment, leading to divorce, disgrace, or death.

moderation *n.* Philosophy whose caution recommends it to the timid and whose dullness is taken for wisdom. Both are at times proved catastrophically wrong, but it remains popular not only among the small and meek but among the great and powerful, who share their sensitivity to criticism. "Liberal journalism," wrote the critic Harold Rosenberg, "assumes that all questions can be solved through 'moderation'—even lies and philistinism must be treated moderately; and this creates a hatred and fear of ideas carried to their conclusion."

modesty *n.* Trait that identifies the wealthy as gentlemanly or ladylike and everyone else as a loser who is not promoting his brand.

Like modesty, diffidence is a reluctance to draw attention to oneself. Outbreaks of diffidence occur when spectators shrink from unseemly self-dramatization, respecting the right of an assailant or vandal to go about his private business without interference.

monkey *n.* Pet kept by the more than usually ironic or the more than usually oblivious. "Monkeys and cats, cats and monkeys, the whole of life is there," said Henry James, who somewhat overstated the case. One occasionally meets a human dog, though his resemblance to the canine may be limited to eating when he is not hungry.

morality *n.* (1) Reason given for refraining from something one didn't want to do anyway. (2) Problem that men delegate to their wives, mothers, or secretaries. As has been often remarked, businesswomen frequently fail to reach the top because they insist on dealing with even petty matters themselves.

mother *n.* Fallen idol. Once inspiring sentiment and reverence, the mother is now acknowledged, in a rare mass application of logic, to partake of all the vices formerly recognized only in the mother-in-law. Saying that you realize that you have become in some way like your mother is a recognized call for sympathy or contradiction. This seems hard on women who have had to manage without servants—as a character in an Angela Thirkell novel says of nannies, they "really make mother-love possible."

Theoretically, the decline of the mother should have led to a corresponding decline in marital conflict. In practice, however, wife and husband are less likely than wife and mother to combine against a common foe.

Though disliking your mother may no longer create guilt, it still leaves an emotional vacancy. While the English find solace in teddy bears, Americans favor female politicians whose program is to kiss it better.

move on *v.* Wish, often coupled with "put this behind me," in which victims of crime, immorality, or negligence ape the dignified detachment of the perpetrator.

movie *n.* Technology that makes it possible to fall in love with a ghost.

A century of movies portraying public and private behavior in all its manifestations has had no effect in promoting self-awareness in viewers. Show any reasonably confident person a film of himself walking, talking, or eating, and watch the blood drain from his face.

multitask *v.* To do three or more things at once (two is normal), none very well. Those who multitask for the entire working day are said to be highly "skilled" or "qualified," though some may simply suffer from a short attention span.

museum *n.* Repository of yesterday's aesthetic standards, regarded with indifference by visitors presented with home accessories they cannot buy. In one art museum in France, visitors are greeted with the statement by the poet Paul Valéry that a man should no more enter a museum without love than he should a woman, a notion clearly irrelevant to the higher standard of living we enjoy today.

narcissism *n.* Basis of all social and professional relations. The delight of Caliban at seeing his face in a glass.

Narcissists get bad press, but they do perform a service. Deciding whether a new acquaintance is worth one's time can be so wearing that, when someone quietly accepts all favors and compliments as his due, we are happy to defer to his judgment.

natural *adj.* Feelings or behavior produced by a lifetime of exposure to propaganda, technology, and literature.

It is widely believed that, while someone or something natural can be made artificial, the reverse is impossible, with one exception. People with the bad luck to have been born elsewhere can be compassionately converted into naturalized citizens.

nature *n.* A great bully, indifferent or hostile to human arrangements and therefore to be circumvented or vanquished.

needs *n.* Items or emotions insistently demanded today, as one did not know of their existence yesterday.

negative growth *n.* Economists' term for the condition that results in positive starvation.

negativity *n.* Reality.

neutral *adj.* Term commonly used to mean "having no opinion," actually meaning, as with neutral Ireland in World War II, "having an opinion"—i.e., that there was no difference between the Nazis and their enemies—"best kept to oneself."

news *n.* Events that, after a certain age, one may find shocking but not surprising and certainly not new.

New Yorker *n.* Inhabitant of a glamorous, independent city-state, discomfited on going abroad to discover he is merely an American.

no *adv.* Monosyllable once taken literally by children but disbelieved by men. Now the reverse is true—at least, among men who fear a lawsuit. The author has heard several mothers say that they never say no because children will disobey anyway, and they do not wish to have their

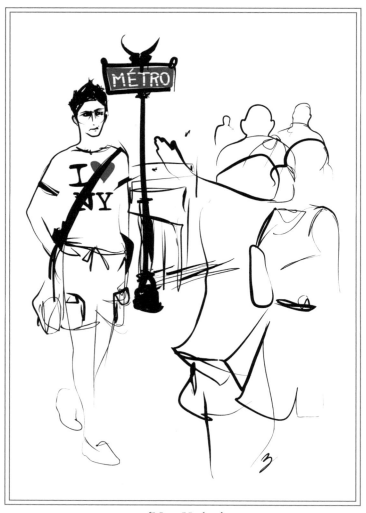

{New Yorker}

authority undermined. Sometimes this is only technically true, as with one who, asked permission to do something by her nine-year-old son, told him, "You must use your own judgment, but personally I wouldn't advise it."

noise *n.* Sound, sometimes called "talk" or "music," that creates the illusion that one is not alone in the world. Conveniently, both types can be found in church.

novel *n.* Story of love, murder, or social climbing meant to assuage the disappointment of those who have been too timid to try these amusements or have failed in them. In its imaginary world, the injustices of this one can be put right, and the misdeeds of sympathetic characters can be explained away. The novel can function as therapy for its author as well as its readers. Think of the number of literary works in which sour, middle-aged college professors of repellent appearance are besieged by young beauties with mattresses on their backs.

nursing home *n.* Prison where children incarcerate their parents, who are thereby given leisure to reflect on their own exercise of power fifty years before.

obesity *n.* Visible compensation for decline in the weight of American power.

obituary *n.* Public notice of the accomplishments of some old person you tolerated, annoyingly brought to your attention too late to boast of the acquaintance.

obliviousness *n.* Quality necessary for maintaining sanity and serenity. See alertness.

occultism *n.* The fascism of idiots. A belief that success derives from secret knowledge and magic powers is fundamental to both. In the optimistic and mild-mannered United States, believers do not read *The Protocols of the Elders of Zion* but best sellers assuring them that intelligence, originality, hard work, or talent are less important than radiating goodwill or memorizing a few simple phrases.

Along with their usefulness to unscrupulous authors, occultists allow the religious and atheists to enjoy a good laugh together. The atheists have an even bigger laugh when they get home.

oeuvre *n.* Not, as some believe, the French for "egg," but the egg-like condition of a life's work, as regarded by critics infatuated with their theories and by dealers with a calm, steady love of their bank balance. Like the *oeuf* served to the sycophant at his boss's house, it will always be found of an oeuvre that "parts of it are excellent." Incompetence, tastelessness, or insanity throughout most of the subject's career is therefore no barrier to study or purchase.

offended *adj.* Right.

officialese *n.* Language spoken by directors of corporations and their public-relations outfits to the public. Intended to convey their superiority to mundane affairs, such as wages and working conditions. When the company president says he is concerned with "shaping a quality environment," he is talking about Impressionist paintings for the office, not pollution that causes cancer.

older *adj.* Old. The trouble with free-floating comparatives is that one is free to supply one's own measure. The author reminds herself, each time she passes the "Home for Older People," that they are understood to be older than middle-aged people, not God.

omniscience *n.* State of knowing all things, possessed by those who are famous for knowing one thing well, such as women renowned for singing or smiling who can advise on medical care and foreign policy.

once *adv.* Never. A first offense is its own defense, or, as the genial Germans say, *Einmal ist keinmal.* (Once is never.)

The experimentally or criminally minded must keep in mind, however, that this leniency cannot be extended. Voltaire: *Une fois, philosophe; deux fois, pédéraste.*

opera *n.* Realistic form of entertainment in which everyone sings to his own music in unintelligible words.

opinion *n.* Point of view conveying the speaker's ignorance and self-satisfaction, corrected only by those whose contempt for him is so great as to breach the rules of courtesy.

The way in which opinion is regarded varies greatly. In genteel cultures, opinion is handed down from one generation to another, swaddled in velvet, and occasionally displayed to universal admiration. In more vivacious ones, the opinion is multiple and mutable, causing observers to wonder whether it is the product of intellectual fertility or lack of principle, and giving rise to such sayings as "Two Jews, three opinions."

optimism *n.* Ignorance and fear with a smiling face. The optimist asks only that the laws of time, motion, and probability be altered in his favor, that others put their money, health, and peace of mind at the service of his amour propre, and that, if inconvenienced, they suffer without complaint. In return, he is welcomed everywhere by those who incline toward optimism but lack his energy or insensibility.

originality *n.* Quality popularly equated with merit. It is not necessary for success in the art world, it has been observed, to be good—only to be bad in a new way. Nor is imitation the mark of the untalented: Picasso said that only little artists borrow. "Great artists steal." This would seem to mean that Damien Hirst is a great artist, but no distinction is perfect.

other *n.* Person making selfish and unnecessary claims on one's time and/or money, e.g., telephone salesperson, charity worker, employer, friend, child, spouse. Quentin Crisp: "Other people are a mistake."

The direct ratio between the distance of others and the severity of one's judgment is neatly expressed in the game of First, Second, Third Person, as in "I hold fast to my principles; you are at times a bit rigid; he is a stubborn pig" or "I am spontaneous and life-loving; you sometimes let your impulsiveness impair your judgment; she is a slut."

parent *n.* Person whose duties were once carried out by falling in with the values of society, now by ignoring or defying them. Role in which ordinary, moral people can partake of an excitement once confined to criminals and bohemians.

Though the child may often resent certain parental practices that caused unhappiness, adults often come to understand that these proceeded from excellent or at least forgivable reasons. The understanding usually occurs around the time the next generation complains of them.

passivity *n.* The most desirable characteristic of the citizen-consumer, who is encouraged to fulfill his craving for self-expression by switching brands.

pathetic *adj.* Formerly, deserving pity; now, in a sterner age, exciting contempt. In an example of the older usage growing into the present one, the playwright Clifford Bax described another writer's work as "pathetic if it were tolerable."

pearl *n.* Jewel that, like many a fortune, began with a bit of dirt. Louise de La Vallière, one of the mistresses of Louis XIV, asked another if her pearl necklace, which fell several inches below her waist, was too long. "Not at all," said Madame de Montespan. "It is merely trying to get back to where it came from."

peasant *n.* Country dweller who can be counted on for a high level of embroidery and anti-Semitism.

pedant *n.* One who not only is right when you are wrong but notices it.

pedophile *n.* One who increases the happiness of those left high and dry by the fashion of speaking politely of and to blacks and homosexuals. Others find him less congenial. As we enrich those who stimulate the taste for relations with children, and our child-rearing practices maximize the opportunity to gratify it, the pedophile judges us not by what we say but what we do. This is never a good way to win friends.

perceived *adj.* Former description of a judgment that pierced the clouds of illusion, now referring to one that is hidden by them, e.g., "There were doubts about Palin's electability and whether her unquestioned charm [could] overcome her perceived lack of political gravitas." With "alleged," the journalist's prophylactic.

person *n.* Word used to disguise gender so as to avoid discrimination. "Elisabeth Vellacott," stated one obituary, "did not have her first one-person exhibition until her mid-sixties."

pessimist *n.* Optimist with a higher success rate. Unlike his cheery brother, he is pleased when things work out well and pleased when they don't. The pessimist's disappointment at getting the smallest slice of the pie is countered by his pleasure at having predicted that he would.

pet *n.* Companion in adversity and obesity.

phlegmatic *adj.* Realizing that nothing is as good or bad as it first seems. After a lifetime observing love matches that end in venomous divorce, and bereavements whose inconsolable relicts take about two weeks to fill the vacancy, the old tend not to empathize with the sorrows and ecstasies of the young, who pity their insensibility.

{pessimist}

piety *n.* One of many dreary duties the rich subcontract to the poor.

platonic *adj.* Synonym for "sexless" or "ideal," a pairing that the young find an oxymoron and the old a tautology.

pleasure *n.* Expression of one's taste, in a way that does not affect others, often more harshly condemned than expressions of one's politics, which do.

Pleasure is always being censured by freelance moralists, who do not seem to realize that, however degrading the pleasure—not only to the pleasure-seeker but those around him—it usually makes money for someone and is therefore socially useful. They cannot, however, be faulted in their objections to pleasures that cause harm to animals or trees.

Plus ça change, plus c'est la même chose **prov.** French phrase that, for accuracy's sake, should have the addition *mais plus cher.*

poetry *n.* Medium in which one says that which is too foolish to say in prose. The King James committee knew what it was doing.

What is too foolish to say in poetry can be set to music.

political correctness *n.* Means of enforcing civilization on the primitive that finds much favor among anti-imperialists and that enables the idle and ignorant to patronize their betters.

The more sensitive advocates of political correctness do not limit their concern to our species. Hence, the term "pet" is discouraged in favor of "companion animal," and the author was once reproved for referring to a baboon in the zoo as a monkey. "Don't say 'monkey,'" said her human companion. "It's not nice. Say 'chimpanzee.'"

politician *n.* Official afflicted with a proleptic form of amnesia, who has no consciousness of the results of his policies, either when they take effect or after he leaves office.

politics *n.* Force that many people believe will take no notice of them if they take no notice of it. A bit like gravity.

portrait *n.* Verbal or visual work that permits us to enjoy with its subject a facsimile of intimacy, usually preferable to the real thing.

positive thinking *n.* Religion without getting up early.

possible *adj.* Irresistible.

posterity *n.* A judge erroneously believed to be the only impartial one.

prayer *n.* Activity pursued by those who believe that, in heaven as on earth, the squeaky wheel gets the grease.

prejudiced *adj.* Experienced.

{politics}

pretentious *adj.* Affecting to possess more money than you see evidence of or more knowledge than you understand.

pride *n.* Self-congratulation on having been the beneficiary of chance or the efforts of others. Demonstrated by the demand of a high price when selling out.

princess *n.* Female whose superiority is established by heredity or baseless conviction. In "The Princess and the Pea," a young woman who turns up at a stranger's home and demands a bed for the night provides further proof of being a princess when she complains bitterly at having been kept awake by a dried pea beneath twenty mattresses. Gratitude and tact are for commoners.

principle *n.* Preference that is tolerated until it causes inconvenience.

prison *n.* One of five institutions, and sometimes six, in which one's incarceration is intended to be lightened by teaching or entertainment, though these sometimes do not make their way into practice. The others are the childhood home, school, workplace, marital home, and nursing home.

privatize *v.* Steal.

problem *n.* **(1)** Failure in intelligence or character that causes one to notice another's stupidity or immorality ("I have a problem with that") or reject an opportunity to make money ("She doesn't have a problem with being paid for sexual services"). **(2)** Hypothetical physical or philosophical difficulty that may prevent one from performing a simple task. Hence the waiter's reassurance when asked for a glass of water—"No problem"—that he is not as infirm or as unwilling to work as he looks.

proverb *n.* Ancient statement of wisdom or advice, now often requiring revision, e.g.:

The child is father to the baby.

Neither a borrower nor a lender be if your religion is a protection racket for the rich.

An ounce of prevention is worth a pound of compensation.

A boy's best friend is his mother's new squeeze.

The wages of sin are whatever you can negotiate.

The hand is quicker than the eye when the banker is dealing the cards.

Crime doesn't pay, but you can work on a contingency basis.

Too many cooks spoil the chances for each one's celebrity.

Don't bite off more than the surgeon can sew back on.

If you can't stand the heat, demand that the company turn on the air-conditioning.

A fool and his money are soon popular.

All work and no play make Jack a good excuse when he says he'll be home late.

The wicked flee when no man pursueth because the cops are busy doing paperwork.

Can a man take fire in his bosom, and his clothes not be burned if they are made of polyester?

People who live in glass houses shouldn't throw pot parties.

There are no atheists in foxholes if they are full of believers who cry, "No room!"

Marry in haste; repent when she says she miscounted.

Look not thou upon the wine when it is red if someone is buying champagne.

A little learning is usually sufficient.

Two's company, three's an extra charge.

There's many a slip 'twixt the cup and the liposuction.

In the kingdom of the blind, the one-eyed can walk around naked.

Two heads are better than one, unless you live next to the nuclear-power plant.

Faint heart never won fair lady or had to worry about a sexual-harassment suit.

He who fights and runs away will find he's left some DNA.

psychoanalyst *n.* One who believes that a problem shared is a problem solved.

psychopath *n.* One oblivious to the consequences of his actions and the feelings of others. Rare condition.

public relations *n.* Profession that, as its name suggests, is a metaphorical version of a much older one.

punctuality *n.* Former virtue that, in the age of the cell phone, has been superseded by flexibility.

{punctuality}

quotation *n.* Means of impressing listeners with one's learning, concealed as humility in repeating another's thoughts rather than expressing one's own. To ensure the acceptance of an idea, however inane, it is necessary only to claim that one is quoting someone the listener admires.

One cannot be sure, however, that even the most brilliant or worthy person will be admired by everyone, or that his exemplary qualities are transferable. "Dr. Johnson is wonderful," said the journalist and critic Auberon Waugh. "But people who quote Dr. Johnson are awful."

rationalization *n.* Product of the intellect's willingness to do the bidding of lust, laziness, vanity, or cowardice. The intellectually deficient are not uniquely shortchanged in this area, as others are willing to do it for them and publicize the result. This is called advertising.

reading *n.* Pastime of the unfit, unpopular, and sexually and patriotically suspect. Americans, said Raymond Chandler, do not seem able to acquire brains without losing blood.

reality *n.* State inhabited by at least some people, certainly the ones whose existence is corroborated by some more reliable means than our eyes, such as television or the Internet. "Let us treat other people as if they are real," said a philosopher. "Who knows—perhaps they are."

reason *n.* A harsh master, usually overthrown by self-justification and appetite. The public does not like reason, said the novelist J. G. Ballard: It is too much like math.

rectitude *n.* A quality that drives one to do the right thing and to ensure that others do it, too, even if this means ignoring the protests not only of those doing the wrong thing but those to whom they are doing it.

reinvent *v.* To repeat, with improvements, your original parthenogenesis so that all trace of your former identity is obliterated. For some, this involves plastic surgery, a change of name, relocation, and a new job. For others, in our inattentive and hyperamnesiac world, it may require only that you color your hair.

The nineteenth-century financier August Belmont, né Schonberg, was walking down Fifth Avenue one day with his friend, a hunchback. "I am going to tell you a secret you may find hard to believe," said the rich man. "Do you know—I used to be a Jew."

"That is a great surprise indeed," said his friend. "And now I will give you an even bigger one. I used to be a hunchback."

relative *adj.* Comparative that the wise remember when faced with a superlative, e.g., "The city government has won an award as the best in the state." As Shaw said, "The least ugly daughter is the family beauty."

relevant *adj.* Of a type of art or entertainment that graciously accommodates itself to the customer rather than rudely asking the reverse.

reminiscence *n.* Self-flagellation. The novelist Elaine Dundy: "If what you're remembering is better than what you have now, it makes you sad that it's gone, and, if it's worse than what you have now, why would you want to remember it?"

remorse *n.* Bitter recollection of missed opportunity for sinning.

repetition *n.* Attempt to impress reader or listener by stealing his time, e.g., "This new discovery reveals for the first time that the two works both shared a great many more qualities in common than was formerly the general consensus." Though as ineffectual as most other methods, it usually makes the writer or speaker too pleased with himself to notice.

reputable *adj*. Discreet.

respect *n*. The idiot's demand for sycophancy, the old person's for agreement, the thug's for servitude.

respectable *adj*. Of a person who is unimaginative, humorless, sexually undesirable, and unfashionably dressed.

responsible *adj*. Of one who insists on full credit and reward for a desirable outcome of his efforts and a purely technical acknowledgment, if any, of having originated a disaster. Upon the discovery of the Watergate burglary, Richard Nixon, ahead of his time in many ways, said that he took the responsibility but not the blame.

retirement *n*. Period of incessant activity to prove to oneself and others that one is not dead.

romantic *adj*. Of a person, sensible. The romantic need only know his heart to follow it and either attain his goal or never be plagued by regret. The pragmatic man, who fears to listen to it, never knows the thrill of courage or of recklessness, as he believes they are the same. If he does not attain his goal, there is no consolation. And, while he is doggedly pursuing what seems a prudent course, his wife has probably eloped with a passing balladeer.

Once offered before the main event as a form of temptation, the romantic gift, event, statement, or other officially recognized evidence of love now tends to be presented afterward, as a form of tribute. It has often been extracted, after much whining and nagging by the wife or partner, to satisfy that perpetual probation officer, her best friend.

Oddly, the word can refer either to that which pertains to love or to that which has no basis in fact. No one knows the reason for this.

rule *n.* Directive obeyed or ignored by the foolish and weak, moderated according to character and circumstance by the brave and clever. The extent to which the Western world's first ten rules of conduct are flouted is heartening evidence of the courage and intellect that surround us.

As the unspoken rules of sensible and courteous behavior have become increasingly ignored or unknown, official rules have increased geometrically to prevent damage to feelings, people, and property. This remedy has been somewhat vitiated by a concomitant decline in the ability to read.

sacrifice *n.* Nobly refusing an opportunity for fame, money, or pleasure that one had little or no chance of acquiring.

schadenfreude *n.* Word that, usually left untranslated, implies that only Germans are guilty of it. Joy in the failings of others, however, is a widespread component of character, as we can see from the television shows that offer numerous and varied examples of the inept and self-deluded for our enjoyment. Discomfort arises when we wonder how many viewers are being inspired by them.

school tax *n.* Demand resented by the childless that reassures them by being low enough to ensure that it will not make the schools good enough for the poor to take their jobs.

secret *n.* Common knowledge, packaged for gain. Secrets abound in the most widely practiced activities, as we can see from the numerous experts who hawk the secrets of making friends, love, or mashed potatoes. The word tactfully absolves those in need of the secret from a lifetime of never having read a book or listened to their mother.

self-contained *adj.* Journalist's description of a good-looking female who, in response to questions, produces after long deliberation, "yes," "no," or, after a thorough search of her intellectual cupboard, "I think so." The definition applies to men, too, as any woman can testify who strikes up acquaintance with the darkly glowering quiet type.

self-effacing *adj.* Desirous of remaining unnoticed, e.g., a young woman in a short, low-cut dress patterned in army camouflage.

self-esteem *n.* Feeling that, unlike self-respect, requires no objective correlative. Despite much time and effort spent inculcating the belief, no one can teach its perquisites: inexperience and a bad memory.

senior citizen *n.* Old person who has never bothered to vote.

S
T

sense of humor *n.* A gift that, if exercised by the poor or powerless, usually keeps them so. If a person possessing it does acquire riches or power, it will most likely disappear, at least in relation to himself. As with those who have inherited these advantages, however, he will be well protected from realizing this.

Humor, as men define it in a woman, is the ability to find a man's jokes enormously funny, a quality distinct from the far less desirable ability to make jokes of her own (showing off) and the unforgivable one of making jokes about him (disrespect). As with intelligence, the humorous woman may be forgiven her flaw if she is sufficiently young, pretty, and pliant, but not for long. A man usually fails to reflect, however, that he judges a woman's sense of humor by whether she makes jokes, especially about him, within earshot.

The more pointed form of humor, wit is even less popular. The great philosopher George Santayana, himself a wit (Protestantism, he said, was a form of inoculation against any real religion), thought it "a merit we should miss little in anyone we love."

sensualist *n.* One whose desire to experience as much pleasure as possible in his earthly span is condemned by those who lack his courage or ingenuity. Denounced as extravagant and selfish, the sensualist often does not appropriate but simply rearranges. Yet how much resentment he incurs for taking the ingredients of the conformist's life of boiled eggs, buttered bread, and milk and making them into French toast!

sentimentality *n.* The superimposition of the ego upon the object—as Norman Mailer put it, "the emotional promiscuity of those who have no sentiment." Those who reflexively grin the biggest and coo the loudest at a puppy under the Christmas tree are often the most difficult to find when it needs a walk, and silent and indifferent when it disappears.

sex *n.* Recreational activity granting instant self-esteem. Only in others does it lead to grave emotional disturbance, loss of money or employment or marital status, unwanted pregnancy, disease, injury, and death. Suitable, therefore, for people of any age past puberty to engage in with any others, without knowing their character, full name, or home address. Not to be confused with such transactions as renting a room or selling homemade pies, which require extensive and complex government intervention.

The spontaneity with which so many embark upon sex these days was not unknown in former times, but the act was often viewed more realistically. Casanova learned this while living in London. Soon after visiting a notorious pleasure garden and pleasuring a stranger, he encountered her at a party. She returned his greeting with a cold stare. "Sir," said the well-born lady, "a gallantry is hardly the same as an introduction."

Though misleadingly passive, the verb "to have sex" is otherwise less misleading than the phrase it has largely replaced. In one of the few retreats from sentimentality, we no longer say that two teenagers in a hurry are "making love." In some media, a form of this genteel fiction persists. One British newspaper, if needing to refer to two young people entwined in an alley, describes them as "a courting couple."

sexual revolution *n.* The time when men of the middle and upper classes began to widen their field of predation from women of the lower class to those of their own.

sex worker *n.* Woman who sells pleasure to a man with no expectation of it for herself. With the increasing standards of women and the decreasing desirability of men, the term may soon be extended to amateurs.

share *v.* Annoy.

shareholder *n.* Person on whose behalf the members of a board have no choice but to hold their noses and perform some distasteful act. That the members are also shareholders is neither here nor there.

shopping *n.* Newest and most popular of the religions, though many consider it an art; in either case, not to be trifled with by the skeptic or dilettante.

The rise of shopping has greatly enriched the lives of those who would otherwise have been at a loss for occupation and conversation, as, unlike the other popular leisure activity among the unskilled, it can be enjoyed without a companion and discussed without embarrassment.

shyness *n.* Unfortunate condition that prevents one from saying something that would give pleasure or from pointing out another's mistake. Its resemblance to selfishness or toadying is only superficial.

Shyness among men has a simple cure, as they often let attractive women know.

silence *n.* Unnatural condition much alleviated by women and children. In public, the proprietors of shops and restaurants kindly provide uninterrupted music, or similar, to allay the worries of those who would otherwise doubt their existence. Individuals who wish to make clear that they live on a higher plane than the rest of us carry with them noises far more interesting than any the world may provide. Removing a device from your ear to answer a question is the contemporary equivalent of lifting a lorgnette.

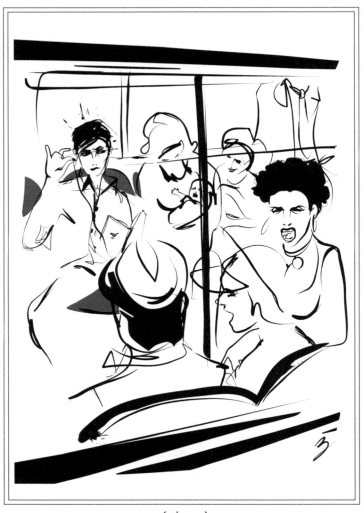

{silence}

The temptation that silence may give to thinking in solitude and to serious conversation in company demonstrates the need for governments and merchants to remain allied, the better to stamp it out.

sliced bread *n.* Purported high-water mark of human happiness, demonstrating a devotion to conformity and manufacturing.

smile *n.* An exposure of the teeth that, in a monkey, is a prelude to attack. Among his descendants, a sign—true or not—that one is benevolently disposed toward another, though some less evolved humans retain the former meaning. Joseph P. Kennedy said of a man at a distance to whom he was baring his teeth: "You know, that guy thinks I'm smiling."

smoke *n.* An indication that there must be, as a character played by Franklin Pangborn remarked in an old film, somebody smoking.

snobbery *n.* A form of irrational worship to which the atheist is as susceptible as the devout.

social Darwinism *n.* The adaptation of the theory of evolution by people proud of at least partly owing their success to their ancestors, who may have acquired their genes through rape or adultery.

Oddly, or perhaps not, many devout believers in social Darwinism indignantly repudiate unmodified Darwinism.

solitary confinement *n.* Punishment for being excessively wicked, virtuous, or old.

solitude *n.* Illness for which many manufacturers can provide cures, and also cures for the cures.

solution *n.* Liquid in which the components of a problem disperse, to regroup soon after in slightly altered form.

source *v.* Of an item in a shop or an ingredient in a product or on a menu, to find what one is seeking, after an arduous and extensive quest, in a land where bright-eyed, clean-limbed natives, living in ecologically sound communities, prepare and package it, while singing traditional, happy songs. Vulgarly: buy.

spontaneity *n.* Of all affectations, the least easily detected by those meant to be fooled, who often include the person practicing it.

stage *n.* Place where, as one actress observed, people say the same thing every night, but, unlike people elsewhere, get paid for it.

stress *n.* Life.

stupidity *n.* Excuse that, used effectively, disarms criticism. "I'm so sorry, I've been extremely stupid," says the educated and well-dressed person, taking the complainer's breath away, and of course not being believed for a minute. Those less favored by nature and fortune can use it, too. If said calmly and clearly while looking the irate person in the eye, it announces his thoughts so plainly that he hastens to deny them, and both parties feel much better than they would after several minutes of one blustering and the other staring at his shoes. Unfortunately, the stupid, living up to their name, seldom realize this.

sublimation *n.* Process by which a repressed desire for work is converted into energy and creativity devoted to sex.

suspicion *n.* Scrutiny we apply to all motives but our own.

swearing *n.* Declaration of fealty to the gods of impotence and rage. Allows children of the middle class and poor to show their elders the contempt shown them in other ways by the rich. Like acting and sex, an activity for which it is popularly but wrongly believed neither talent nor experience is necessary.

The general acceptance of swearing, even by children and before strangers, was thought to herald a new world of democratic discourse. It has, however, created a society in which safety from verbal assault is guaranteed only to the physically or financially powerful.

talk *v.* To convey information and ideas orally to someone who usually will not listen, probably not understand, most likely not care, and definitely not remember.

taste *n.* Quality whose value in personal relations is much overrated, as many have found when the loved one, who likes all the same books, films, food, and music, bounces a coffeepot off their head. As Queen Elizabeth II is reported to have said, sadly, of taste, "It doesn't help." Americans are often surprised to learn, if they ever do, that taste cannot be bought and that bad taste is considered, in some far from lowly circles, superior to no taste at all—or what the poet John Betjeman called "ghastly good taste."

Those who lack money might trouble our consciences unduly if we could not use their atrocious taste to affirm our superiority. Though most people consider it wrong to laugh at someone clothed in rags, one may laugh at the less impoverished whose clothing bears the name of a company or sports team. People so amused often demonstrate their own good taste by wearing the name of a Frenchman or Italian who is laughing at them.

tattoo *n.* Literature inscribed on people in inverse proportion to its presence in their homes. As the romantic and impetuous often find, it can make the skin the graveyard

{tattoo}

of affections that have not survived the fluctuations of the more mutable organs.

Unlike concentration-camp inmates, present-day wearers of tattoos have been branded voluntarily to indicate they have no future.

tea *n.* Meal that, not requiring the skill of cooking, the expense of alcohol, or the obligation to entertain others for very long, exemplifies English hospitality.

teamwork *n.* Means of encouraging a taste for solitude and a suspension of disbelief. Team members are required to believe that all are on the same side against rival entities, rather than each against one another, and that success depends on cooperation rather than competition or consanguinity.

tease *v.* Of a child, to be impertinent or cruel. Of a pretty woman who has made an effort not to look like a walking laundry bag, to promise sexual favors falsely.

terrorism *n.* Source of self-regard. While the cell phone merely allows individual big boys to imagine themselves policemen, firemen, brain surgeons, or in some other way indispensable, terrorism enables entire companies of them, defended by elaborate security systems, to do so.

Thanksgiving *n.* Native Americans' revenge.

think *v.* Feel.

tip *n.* Remuneration for service given a waiter in proportion to the bill, this being considered representative of his effort, since carrying the expensive bottle of wine he has recommended weighs more heavily on his conscience than a cheaper one.

tolerant *adj.* Drunk.

trademark *n., adj.* Like "signature," unique characteristic or mode of behavior by which individual brands of the product *Homo sapiens* may be recognized—e.g., "The Revolutionary United Front, whose trademark was the amputation of the hands of innocent civilians"; "He greeted the voters with his trademark smile."

Tradition *n.* The god of doing nothing, as opposed to Chastity, the god of nothing doing. Tradition decrees that, if something has been done for a long time, only laziness, stinginess, or spite could motivate anyone trying to abolish or change it. The Spanish movement to ban bullfighting is puzzling to those who do not see why a distinctive national tradition should be abandoned—after all, the bulls don't buy tickets.

tragedy *n.* In the world, frustration of expected victory or perfection. In the theater, drama in which the protagonist, curiously, comes to disaster through an excess of self-expression.

travel *v.* To remove yourself to a faraway place where people behave in an entirely different way than they do at home, in which case you may laugh at them, or behave in the same way, in which case you may, without loss of reputation, join them.

traveler *n.* Tourist with money, susceptible to parting from it when so addressed.

truth *n.* A crude weapon, used only by those deficient in money or charm, the far more effective techniques of persuasion. Useless against love or other form of stubbornness.

T-shirt *n.* Garment of mass-produced irony, frequently displaying an offer whose acceptance would make the wearer call a policeman.

{truth}

ultimate *adj.* Latest and most expensive, promoted as being the last and best.

unacceptable *adj.* More condemnatory version of inappropriate. Used by people by whom the offender has no wish to be accepted.

uncanny *adj.* Displaying intelligence, taste, or talent, even on a modest scale, that, to writers devoid of these gifts, appears supernatural. "H. P. Lovecraft, who had an uncanny ability to synopsize entire literary careers in a few sentences . . ."

understand *v.* (1) Agree. To dismiss the most erudite and logical objections, one need only smile pityingly and say, "You don't get it, do you?" (2) To absolve of blame, as in "We have to understand the suicide bombers" or "My wife doesn't understand me." The corresponding complaint is never made by women, who know that understanding is irrelevant or inimical to loving. Understanding is a quality more common in the young, as many husbands who complain of not being understood recognize by marrying a second wife half the age of the first. (3) To predict how another will behave, especially in ways that are banal or discreditable. For some people, this is the nearest they can come to love, for which they consider it a superior substitute. (4) To express compassion silently for those who are martyrs to the ease with which their bad tempers are ignited. Often commanded by wives on behalf of their husbands: "I'm afraid you have to understand—Carl can't bear to hear that mentioned." (5) To recognize that the inferiority complex, military-industrial complex, or other abstraction motivates the behavior of every country, institution, individual, cat, and dog. The strenuousness with which some deny this (the cats are particularly indignant) shows how much the truth hurts. (6) To have learned the basic facts about computers, medicine, and other fields that have not changed in the past twenty years. (7) To demonstrate insensitivity or acquaintance with low life. "I cannot understand how anyone can fail to be moved by the final minutes of this show."

U
V

unfashionable *v.* Characteristic of art, jewelry, or antiques you wish to sell, especially to those from whom they were bought. Acquired immediately after purchase.

uvula *n.* Part of the body seen, until recently, only by doctors and voice teachers. Now exhibited, in moments of boredom and fatigue, to all members of the public as a consequence of the increasingly feeble nature of the jaw and of the elbow joint, which once would have raised a covering hand to the mouth. This behavior has been known, however, to revive briefly in proximity to people of greater wealth or influence.

vanity *n.* Exaggerated self-satisfaction about accomplishments, talents, or traits, including one's lack of vanity. The vain would rather be disparaged by the great than praised by the lowly. "I had the misfortune of not being in favor with the duchess [of Argyle]," wrote James Boswell. "She said with some sharpness, 'I *know nothing* of Mr. Boswell.' Poor Lady Lucy Douglas, to whom I mentioned this, observed, 'She knew *too much* of Mr. Boswell.' I shall make no remark on her grace's speech. I indeed felt it as rather too severe; but when I recollected that my punishment was inflicted by so dignified a beauty, I had that kind of consolation which a man would feel who is strangled by a *silken cord.*"

vegetarian *n.* Person who wishes to feel the glow of purity without the drawbacks of the real thing.

veil *n.* Garment that hides from a man the beauty of another man's wife and, from other men, the ugliness of his own.

violence *n.* Activity reserved by some religions for their Supreme Being and by others, more democratically, encouraged in their followers. In civilized societies, violence is carefully regulated, some of the few allowable reasons being self-defense, orders from the government to kill foreign strangers, and the necessity to keep customers entertained.

{vanity}

Responsible parents ensure that, if a film is rated less than universally acceptable, the reason is violence, rather than sex, which sets a far worse example. Foreigners predictably believe the opposite. In England, parents are warned if a film "contains mild peril."

virtue *n.* Complex compound of various types of activity, such as refraining from sex with a person you do not like or consistently doing the minimum amount of work necessary to fulfill job requirements.

vulnerable *adj.* Too fragile to be apprised of fault and misbehavior, a quality the vulnerable ensure is made clear to the most casual observer.

waiter *n.* Superior being whose ability to carry trays without, usually, dropping them makes even the most belligerent egalitarian feel inadequate. The modern waiter dispels this awe and serves notice that criticism or poor tipping would be an insult to his friendliness by greeting a male, female, or mixed group with "Hi, guys!" No woman, no matter how feminist, would dare dispute this gender reassignment, considering what we know goes on in the kitchen.

war *n.* Means of providing employment for the poor, profit for the wealthy, and indignation for the middle class.

wedding *n.* Festival of female glorification that ends with the woman and her betrothed pronounced mother and child. During the ceremony, the bride's and groom's families range themselves on either side of the aisle, taking the battle positions they will retain for the duration of the marriage.

well liked *adj.* Admired, respected, regarded with affection—or so one believes who has never quietly returned to collect his umbrella.

{wedding}

widow *n.* Obsolete term for a female who, having known the sexual embraces of a man, is presumed eager for their repetition by another. The present term is "woman."

In its former meaning, the word gave rise to the term "merry widow." It was never suggested that the lady might owe her merriment to her solitary state.

will *n.* Means of purchasing courtesy and respect on the installment plan. At times a greatly prolonged joke by those not previously suspected of a sense of humor.

women's magazine *n.* Periodical in which half the articles tell how to trap a man, the other half how to put up with him, purchased by readers who have not come to the obvious conclusion.

wrinkle *n.* Line indicating character on the face of a man or impoverished woman.

xenophobe *n.* Backward person who does not realize that wealthy or influential foreigners are quite different from the rest.

Yiddish *n.* Language, created in a time of persecution, in which many words can mean their opposite, so that Jews could deliver insults or offer warnings without fear of retribution. "He is a *chochem,*" for example, means that the person is scholarly and wise. "He is a *chochem,*" on the other hand, means that the person is an idiot. That should clear things up.

youth *n.* Period of happiness and promise, infinitely extendable by surgery, celebrity, immaturity, or personal comparison.

About the Author

Rhoda Koenig was born in New York City, where she was for many years the book reviewer of *New York* magazine. She has written for *Harper's, The New York Times, The New Republic, The New York Review of Books,* and *Vogue.* She lives in London, where she has written social commentary and book, art, and theater reviews for many publications, including *The Independent, The New Statesman, The Spectator, The Times, The Times Literary Supplement, The Evening Standard, The Daily Telegraph,* and *Private Eye.*

About the Illustrator

Peter Breese's illustrations and artwork have appeared in a variety of publications, including *Spectrum 18, They Draw & Cook, Me: In focus, Covet,* and *Ballad Of.* His work has been exhibited in galleries in Los Angeles, Dallas, Denver, Ann Arbor, and Key West, and his clients range from fashion boutiques to Hollywood stars. He lives in Ann Arbor, Michigan, with his wife and two children.